The Blokes Book of Cooking

Errol J van Blerk

The Blokes Book of Cooking
Sydney, Australia

A CIP catalogue record of this book is available from the National Library of Australia

ISBN 978-0-9943950-2-3

Disclaimer

While every care has been taken in compiling the The Blokes Book of Cooking, the author, or any other persons who have been involved in working on this publication, cannot accept responsibility for any errors or omissions, however inadvertent, that may be found in the recipes or text, nor for any problems that may arise as a result of preparing one of these recipes.

November 2015

Published by MAEJ-IC Pty Ltd

Sydney, Australia

Acknowledgement

I would like to thank Myra-Ann, Elisa-Marie, Maegan and Brenden for their willingness to try almost everything that I have ever made and for encouraging me even through the real lows such as my avocado soup, may it rest in peace.

Contents

Introduction

My first cooking attempts were not award winners, but I learned a lot as I tried things. My wife and oldest daughter went through my 'bread crumb' period where everything was crumbed whether it should have been or not. However, by the time our next two kids came along, I had a working knowledge of all the kitchen tools, how to read a recipe and I had made friends with my stove, oven and microwave.

All the cookbooks though, seemed to be written for people whose mothers had trained them in the basics, or maybe cooking was just genetically encoded.

This book is for blokes who have never really paid much attention to the kitchen before. It is for those out on their own for the first time, or those newly divorced or widowed and whose mums, wives or partners always did the cooking.

It's also for those blokes who would just like to learn how to cook and don't have much idea how to get started.

The common view of blokes is that they won't ask for directions, read the manual or admit that they need help. This is the basic blokes book of cooking which will reduce the need to do any of the above. It does require that you read it when you are stuck, or if you want to impress with your skills and knowledge. You don't have to admit to ever having read this book or even that you have seen it. Regard it as a secret weapon and the more closely we can guard this secret, the better.

And by the way there are no pictures of any of the completed dishes on purpose. When I started cooking I often felt demotivated by the perfect looking picture in the book, and my result looked nothing like it. So, don't worry about it right now. Whatever you produce will be perfect!

Few of the recipes are complicated and the majority of them can be made with little or no cooking experience. All of the recipes have been tested on my friends and family and no one suffered any negative consequences in their development.

Things you ought to know

This chapter is full of the basic definitions and tools for creating a working relationship with your kitchen and the food in it.

Tools of the Trade

Unlike working on a car, there are very few special tools required for cooking - and you still get to use the cook's equivalent of power tools such as blenders and mixers. In addition, you have the opportunity to play with sharp knives and to work on hot surfaces.

Now I know that most blokes like hardware stores or electronics stores because of all the neat stuff. Well here is your chance to find out how much fun the kitchen section of your nearest department store is or, better yet, one of those speciality kitchen stores. You'll need a basic tool kit to get started: (Numbers in brackets refer to illustrations in the picture.)

Mixing Bowls (1) – nothing fancy – a set of inexpensive stainless steel ones from Kmart will do. They're easy to use, easy to clean and if you drop them, they go clang rather than crash tinkle.

Spatter Guard (2) – useful for placing over the frying pan when cooking to stop oil and grease from being spattered all over the stove top.

Cutting Board (3)

Set of Sharp Knives (4) – this should include a carving knife and sharpening steel.

Cheese Grater (5) – preferably one that has fine, medium and coarse options.

Double Boiler (6) – usually consists of two saucepans that fit together. The bottom saucepan is filled with water and the top saucepan is filled with a mixture requiring non-direct heat to prepare. Sometimes they also come with a steamer insert which is used in place of the upper pot for steaming.

Saucepans (7) – 1 (1qt), 2 (2qt), 3 (3qt) and 8 (8qt) litre (preferably stainless steel).

Colander (8) – for draining vegetables and pasta after cooking.

Frying Pans (9) – non-stick (handy to have two).

Wire Rack (10) – a wire rack for cooling stuff like biscuits and cakes.

Mortar and Pestle (11) – for grinding up herbs and spices.

Sifter (12) – this can be as simple as a smaller version of what you use for sifting sand to something with a handle on the side that you wind.

Set of Measuring Spoons (13)

Set of Measuring Cups (14)

Can Opener (15)

Microwave Cookware (16) – usually plastic, or ceramics that are labelled as microwave safe, because putting metal in a microwave can cause permanent damage to it.

Tongs (17)

Whisk (18)

General Utensils (19) – such things as a vegetable peeler, spatula, slotted spoon, spaghetti spork ( you have to love the creativity of the name; spoon + fork = spork. In my house, it's known as a 'spaghetti picker-upper').

Various Sized Spatulas – we used to call them pot lickers when I was a kid because, if you used one to clean the pot or bowl, there was nothing left to lick. Another term I've heard is a 'meanie' for the same reason.

Wooden Spoons – wooden spoons are ideal for stirring most things because they don't scratch or mark your pots and pans. When folding in frothy things like beaten egg whites a metal spoon is best because it won't knock as much air out of the mixture.

Oven Mitt/Pot Holder – I know the tough-guy thing to do is to lift hot things with your bare hands. The problem is that treating the burns takes time and you'd need to figure this into the timing for your recipes.

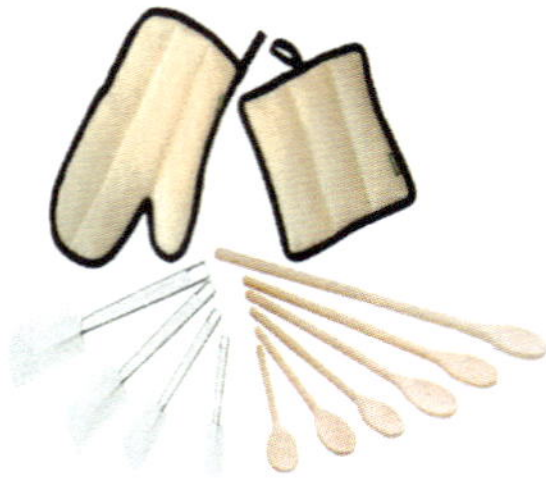

Rolling Pin – this can be either a proper rolling pin or simply a wine bottle (minus the label) full of wine or water to give it some weight, and with the stopper in it, so it doesn't leak.

Brush – for scrubbing the dirt off potatoes.

Pastry Brush – for 'painting' pastry with butter/milk/egg white or for basting (painting oil or butter on a roast).

Piping Bag – basically this is a bag into which you put squishy stuff that you want to squeeze out into a pattern - frosting or icing for example. The cheapest form is a zip lock bag with the corner snipped off, though you can buy a proper one at the shops.

The power tools that would be useful but can be worked around to some degree are:

Mixer – either freestanding (preferable) or hand held.

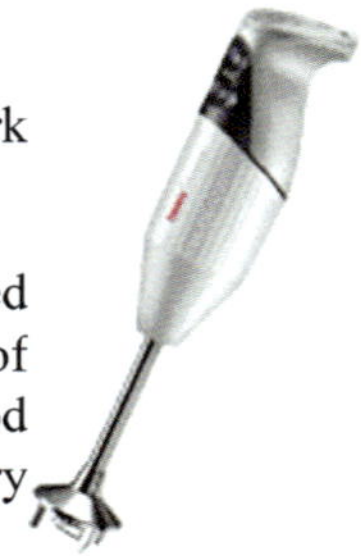

Blender – some freestanding mixers have blender attachments that work fine.

Kitchen Whiz or Bamix – hand held device with a small high-speed blade – useful for pureeing foods (see Jargon section for a definition of pureeing). It's also really dangerous if handled carelessly – almost as good as a circular saw or angle grinder in terms of danger level. A must for every kitchen adventurer.

Extra items that make life easier, but can be done without:

Oven Thermometer – this can be very useful for making sure that your oven is at the right temperature when you're baking. I have often found that the average domestic oven doesn't have a very accurate temperature control. For example, my current gas oven, when set to 180 degrees, gives a centre oven temperature of 160 degrees. Having an oven thermometer has helped me take the guesswork out of getting the temperature right.

Temperature Probe – for testing the inner temperature of cooking foods. It's particularly useful when cooking meat. There is nothing more disappointing than carving into a piece of roasted meat and finding that it's either not cooked enough or, worse still, it's cooked too much.

Having a temperature probe will help to minimise this. There are two basic types of meat probes. The first is what is known as 'instant'. This type of probe is inserted in the meat to take a temperature reading and then removed and the meat is then returned to the oven. The second type is 'oven proof' and is placed in the meat and left there while the meat is in the oven thus giving a continuous reading.

No two people will have an identical list of what you should start out with in your cupboards. It's entirely dependant on your food tastes and your level of interest in your kitchen adventure. The recipes in this book use basics only. In addition to the list below, you'll need to have on hand daily grocery items such as milk, eggs, cheese, etc.

Necessities

Aluminium foil (Alfoil)
Baking paper
Baking powder
Beef stock cubes
Bicarbonate of soda (Bicarb, or Baking Soda)
Black pepper (either ground or in peppercorns. If it's in the form of peppercorns, you'll need a pepper mill or grinder of some sort)
Brown sugar
Caster sugar (Powdered sugar)
Chicken stock cubes
Cornflour (Cornstarch)
Curry powder
Dish washing detergent
Hand soap (See Hygiene)
Mustard
Olive oil
Paper towel
Plain flour
Rice – Arborio (for risottos)
Rice – Long grain
Rolled oats
Salt
Self-raising flour
Sponge and scourer
Sugar
Tea towels
Tomato sauce
Vanilla essence
Vegetable stock cubes

Selection of Herbs and Spices

Apart from guidance that recipes might give, the use of herbs and spices is really dependent on your tastes. A word of caution when experimenting with herbs and spices: try adding a little at a time and tasting between additions. I have managed to render many a good dish inedible because I didn't take this advice. As a guide, the following is a list of herbs and spices and some of the foods with which they work well.

Bay leaves: soups and stews, grilled meats
Cayenne pepper: savoury baked goods, cheese dishes
Chives: salads, vegetables, potatoes, eggs
Cinnamon: baked goods, fruits, beverages
Cloves: baked goods, hearty meats
Curry powder: Indian dishes
Ginger: baked goods, Asian dishes, vegetables
Italian mixed herbs: spaghetti, meat loaf
Mint: beverages, meats, desserts
Mustard: fish, eggs, cheese, meats, sauces
Nutmeg: baked goods, spinach, dairy products
Paprika: Spanish dishes, potatoes, meats
Parsley: salads, soups, meats, fish, stuffing
Pepper: meats, soups and stews, nearly everything
Poppy seeds: baked goods, noodles, salad dressings

Rosemary: chicken, potatoes, stuffing
Sage: poultry, pork, stuffing
Sesame seeds: baked goods, Asian dishes, cheese
Tarragon: chicken, salads, seafood
Thyme: meats, soups and stews, vegetables, stuffing
Vanilla (Vanilla essence): baked goods, beverages

Niceties

Dark Chocolate for cooking – please note that this is not cooking chocolate. A good quality dark chocolate will produce better results when used in cooking than the cheap stuff or the cooking variety. It's also better for sampling while you're cooking.

Orange Essence	Golden Syrup
Lemon Essence	Honey
Icing Sugar	Dark Treacle

Jargon

Some terms it would be useful to know are:

Alfoil – Sometimes known as tin-foil, aluminium foil is used for lining dishes and pans, covering food to keep in the moisture, to cook in and to keep food warm.

Baking Paper – Nonstick paper such as Glad Bake which is used in baking to stop cakes, biscuits, etc. from sticking to the pans, trays, and tins.

Baking Sheet – Also known as a cookie sheet or biscuit sheet. This is a flat pan with little or no sides and they range in size from 22cm x 28cm (9in x 11in) to 32cm x 32cm (12½in x 12½in). The size really doesn't matter, as long as they fit in your oven.

Beat – Vigorously mixing with a fork, whisk or electric mixer with the intention of trapping air in the mixture.

Creaming – This is usually required when a light and airy mixture is needed, in such things as biscuits or cookies. By taking butter that is at room temperature (still firm but not hard) and beating it using a mixer, the texture will change until it looks like thick cream.

Diced – Cut into cubes. The recipe will usually specify the size of the cubes required.

Kneading – Kneading strengthens the gluten and makes for lighter and fluffier bread. This is the process whereby dough is worked with the hands (See section on Hygiene) by folding, pushing and turning the dough until it is elastic (6 to 8 minutes).

Lightly Beaten – Using a fork or whisk, beat an egg until a uniform colour has been achieved.

Lukewarm – When you stick your finger in it the temperature is about the same as if you had put your finger in your mouth. (It's important to wash your hands before you do the mouth test and before you handle any more food. (See section on Hygiene)

Mash – Usually applied to vegetables such as potatoes or pumpkin, it's the process of crushing the food to produce a smooth and even texture.

Mortar and Pestle – A kitchen tool that consists of a bowl (mortar) and a bat-like tool (pestle) that's used to grind spices, herbs and other foods.

Nonreactive Saucepan – A nonreactive saucepan is one that's made from stainless steel, glass, or ceramic materials. They're called nonreactive because these materials don't react with acidic ingredients in the same way as copper and aluminium.

Pinch – Literally a small amount (between thumb and forefinger).

Poach – A method in which items are cooked gently in simmering liquid.

Puree – To blend, sieve, or mash a food until it's very smooth and has the consistency of baby food.

Sauté – To cook food quickly in a small amount of fat or oil, until brown, in a skillet or sauté pan over direct heat. The sauté pan and fat must be hot before the food is added, otherwise the food will absorb oil and become soggy.

Scalded Milk – Milk that has been brought to the boil and put aside to cool.

Set – When applied to a roast it's the process whereby the meat is kept in a warm place for 15 to 20 minutes, after it has finished roasting, to allow the cooking to finish and the juices to settle. When applied to custard, jelly etc., it's the process of allowing the liquid to cool and become semi-solid.

Sieve – To force food through a strainer in order to produce a smooth and even, baby food-like, substance.

Simmer – To cook by bringing liquid to the boil and then reducing the heat so that the surface of the liquid just moves.

Soft Peaks – When the whisk or beater is removed from the beaten egg whites, a peak forms then folds over (see Tips And Techniques).

Sliced – Cut into slices, as with sliced bread.

Stiff but not dry – When the whisk or beater is removed from the beaten egg whites, a peak forms but doesn't fold over (see Tips And Techniques).

Stock – Stock means the broth of vegetables, meat, poultry or fish, and is used in making sauces, soups, gravies and many other dishes. One stock cube or one level teaspoon of stock powder to one cup of water makes one cup of stock. Stock cubes and powder come in three basic flavours: beef, chicken and vegetable.

Tepid – See lukewarm.

Tinfoil – See Alfoil.

Whisk – To whip or quickly beat, usually using a wire kitchen tool called a whisk or, at its simplest, a fork. A wire whisk will aerate better than a fork, making whatever you're working on lighter and fluffier (see Beat above).

Zest – The outer part of the lemon skin or orange skin (yellow/orange part of the peel only), grated fine and used as a flavouring agent or garnish.

Hygiene

When you work on your car, it really doesn't matter if you don't wash your hands before you start, or if you leave some grease on your tools. This isn't the case with cooking. Food poisoning can occur if you don't follow some basic rules.

1. Wash your hands before you start.
2. Wash your tools in hot soapy water after you've finished using them.
3. Keep work surfaces and cutting boards clean (wash down with hot soapy water before and after each use.)
4. Don't drink out of the milk, wine, juice, or beer bottle that you're going to use in your recipes.
5. Wash your hands after you go to the bathroom, pet the dog, sneeze, blow your nose, or scratch your places that might itch from time to time. (Please make sure that you turn your head away from the food if you have to sneeze, cough or any other activity that might cause spray.)
6. If you cut yourself, stop what you're doing and get a band-aid or medical help, depending on the severity of the injury. It's not a good look to bleed into the food that you're preparing.
7. Keep other people who haven't done the above away from your food preparation area.

Testing Raw Ingredients

If the ingredients you're using are stale, rancid, rotting, mouldy, or just plain off you might not be satisfied with your results, so here are a few simple guidelines.

Meat – If the meat smells off then it's probably off and should be thrown away. Furthermore, if it's slimy and green it's probably off and should be thrown away.

Milk – If the milk smells off, or worse yet has lumps in it, it's probably off and should be thrown away.

Eggs – Eggs can be a bit tricky. While they might look OK from the outside, they could be in bad shape internally. The first test is to place the egg in cold water to see if it floats. If it does then throw it away, taking care not to break it because it won't smell great. Another simple precaution with eggs is to break the number called for in your recipe one at a time into a separate glass before pouring it into your mixture. That way if one of them is bad it won't contaminate the rest.

Cheese – Cheese that's mouldy must be approached with caution, with the exception of bleu cheese, which is supposed to be mouldy. If it's light surface mould that has happened as a result of being touched by human hands, then it can be cut off and the remainder used normally. If, however, the mould is as a result of poor refrigeration or poor handling (as if it was dropped on the floor or sneezed on or handled after a visit to the bathroom without hand washing) the cheese should be thrown away. Whenever handling cheese it's important that your hands are clean (see section on Hygiene) and that the touching is kept to a minimum.

Dried Fruit and Nuts – Tasting a small amount is the quickest way to establish the freshness of these ingredients. If they taste off or rancid, they probably are so throw them away.

Packaged Items – Packaged items and products will normally have a 'use-by-date' or a 'freshest before' date. If these dates have passed then it's a good idea not to use them without checking them first.

Chocolate – Tasting some is imperative to ensure that it's OK. (I find no shortage of volunteers for taste testing chocolate.) The same can be said for any alcohol that's planned to be used in the cooking. Just remember moderation in all things – except, (according to the author of The Great Australian Diet, Dr John Tickell) laughter, sex vegetables and fish.

Flour, Corn, Rolled Oats, etc. – If things are alive and building little colonies in these items then it's time to buy some fresh ingredients. After relocating the colony, be sure to wash any containers thoroughly with hot water and soap before re-use.

Fresh Fruit and Vegetables – If it looks bad, smells bad and tastes bad it's probably bad. Depending on the environment in which they're stored, fruits and vegetables can either dry up and become a mummified reminder of what they once were or they go to liquid. Before getting to liquid, the fruit or vegetable will generally pass through a number of interim stages and these might include discolouration on the skin, change to a less attractive colour than the healthy item, production of an unpleasant odour, the growth of a variety of moulds, and many variations on these possibilities.

I'm sure most of you have seen the stages of evolution of a banana. They start out green, thick skinned and very firm. Then they start to turn yellow and become a little softer and the skin starts to thin. Next black starts to appear on the skin and the contents become even softer. The whole thing starts to shrink. Next comes the seeping of internal fluids as the skin becomes even thinner and the flesh starts to become quite mushy. If you haven't thrown it away before this point then you're in for a treat when you pick it up.

I'm sure you get the point. Fresh fruit and vegetables need to be consumed while they're still fresh, while they still hold the vitamins, minerals and other nutrients that you bought them for in the first place.

Separating an Egg

You can always cheat and purchase a plastic egg-separator. If you don't think it's worth it, follow these simple steps to separate your egg yolks from their whites:

1. Crack the egg lightly, as close to the middle as possible, being careful not to break the yolk.
2. Hold half the shell, with the yolk in it, in one hand, and the other half-shell in the other.
3. Allow as much of the egg white as possible to run out of the shell and down into a bowl, then transfer the yolk to the other half of the shell, in the process allowing more of the white to run out.

It should not be necessary to perform this transfer more than twice to get the yolk almost completely clear of egg white. The process is a little awkward, however, and takes some practice. Until you get the hang of it, it's a good idea to have extra eggs on hand, in case the first few tries are less than successful.

There is another way. A bit messy, but what the hey, this is a blokes book of cooking. Simply break the egg into your hand (which is clean – see section on Hygiene) and hold it over a small bowl, then let the egg white run through your fingers. When most of the white has run through your fingers, tip the yolk into a separate bowl. If you have a number of eggs to separate this is possibly the quickest way to go.

If you want to keep the yolks, it doesn't matter very much if one breaks. If you want to keep the whites, it's necessary to be much more careful. Use one bowl to keep the whites in that are already separated, and a different bowl over which to separate the current egg. A little white in the yolks doesn't matter, but a fleck of egg yolk can make a batch of egg whites unusable, because the fat in an egg yolk will stop the whites from fluffing up when they're whipped.

Working with Egg Whites

There are a number of stages that egg whites go through when they're beaten, and recipes will usually define what is needed. It should be noted that, in working with egg whites, it's important that beaters and bowls are clean and dry. Otherwise the whites won't foam up and hold their shape properly. For best results, egg whites should be at room temperature, though they can be used straight from the fridge.

Soft Peaks – the foam is white, shiny and flowing. When the beater or whisk is lifted out of the mixture, small peaks will form and they will immediately fold over at the top.

Stiff Peaks – the foam has reached its maximum size. When the beater or whisk is lifted out of the mixture, small peaks will form and hold their shape. If you cut the foam with a knife, a narrow groove forms with stiff walls.

Stiff and Dry (over-beaten) – the foam is no longer shiny. It's dry and clumpy. This isn't a useful state and if you've reached this point your only option is to start again with some more eggs.

Folding In – a gentle process best done with a metal spoon because a wooden spoon will tend to break more bubbles and force the air out of the mixture. Pour the heavier mixture gently onto the beaten egg whites and then gradually combine the mixture by using long gentle strokes, drawing the mixture from the bottom of the bowl up and over the top. Turn the bowl a little after each stroke. Keep folding the mixture until there are no streaks.

Thickening

When making stews and hearty soups it's sometimes necessary to create a thicker consistency and the way to do this is to add a little milk or water to one tablespoon of cornflour, in a small bowl or cup, and stir until you have a smooth paste. Add the liquid a little at a time until you get the consistency you want. Then add the liquid to the simmering food you want to thicken. Be sure to stir thoroughly while adding the cornflour-liquid mixture. Failure to do this will result in a lumpy sauce. Not a good look.

Testing Cakes for 'doneness'

One of the challenges when baking cakes is trying to judge when they're completely cooked. If they're taken out of the oven too soon, the centre will probably collapse and be quite doughy. Leave them in too long and they start to burn. Neither is a desirable outcome.

The most common methods for testing are:

Skewer or toothpick test – stick a skewer or toothpick into the centre of the cake and if it comes out clean, the cake is cooked. If it comes out with some dough on it, then leave it in for another 5 minutes and test again.

Light touch on the top – by lightly touching the top centre of the cake, the indentation left by your finger should spring back if the cake is cooked. If it doesn't spring back, leave it in the oven for another 5 minutes and test again.

When testing breads and bread rolls for doneness, you're looking for a golden brown crust with a hollow sound when tapped on the top.

Whipping Cream

The easiest place to start is to buy thickened cream from your supermarket because it will produce a nice firm cream when whipped. A word of caution: cream will turn into a butter-like substance if you whip for too long so keep an eye on it.

When using whipped cream as a filling in cakes, and with some desserts, a little caster sugar and vanilla essence can be added to enhance the flavour.

For best results make sure that the beater and bowl are completely clean before you start.

Measuring Ingredients

When a recipe calls for a particular measure it means not packed down so be careful not to push down on the ingredients as you gather them. If a packed measure is required, the recipe will tell you that. For example you'll often see brown sugar as packed. On the other hand you'll sometimes see flour as "sifted". The measure is taken after the sifting process. Sifting is primarily to aerate the dry ingredient.

Cup and Spoon Measures

1/4 cup	=	60ml
1/3 cup	=	80ml
1/2 cup	=	125ml
1 cup	=	250ml
1/4 tsp	=	1.25ml
1/2 tsp	=	2.5ml
1 tsp	=	5ml
1 tblsp	=	20ml

Note: tsp = teaspoon
tblsp = tablespoon

Always use a level measure unless otherwise stated. The easiest way to get a level measure is to scoop up a heaped measure and then, using the back of a straight knife across the rim of the measuring cup or spoon, push off the excess.

One measure that gives international confusion is the quantity of a tablespoon. In the USA, UK and some other parts of the world one tablespoon is equivalent to three teaspoons whereas in Australia, New Zealand and some other places a tablespoon is equivalent to four teaspoons.

All tablespoon references in this book are to the latter. ie a tablespoon = 20ml or four teaspoons.

Pinch – as in a pinch of salt – the amount that you pinch-up between your thumb and forefinger.

Dash – as in a dash of milk – just about what you might put in someone's coffee if they asked to have it with a little milk.

Splash – see dash.

Sprinkle – a bit like a pinch but spread out.

Dollop – as in a dollop of cream – somewhere between a heaped teaspoon and a heaped tablespoon – definitely depends on your own taste.

Oven Temperatures

Convection and fan-forced ovens cook differently. No two of them are the same. This means that even though the control on the front might read 180°C there are no guarantees that any part of your oven will be at that temperature. The best way to deal with this is to buy a good quality oven thermometer, the type that either stands on or hangs from a shelf.

Be aware that fan-forced ovens usually cook faster, and the cooking temperature should be lowered by 10°C.

Another area that can sometimes cause confusion is the whole cooking temperature thing. Some recipes talk in terms of 'moderate' or 'hot' etc. while other recipes will talk degrees. All oven temperatures in this book are in °C.

Oven Temperatures

Description	***°C***	***°F***
Very Slow	120	250
Slow	150	300
Moderately Slow	160	320
Moderate	180	355
Moderately Hot	190	375
Hot	200	400
Very Hot	230	450

Roasting Temperatures and Times

It's also important to know how long and what at temperature to roast meat. As mentioned earlier, experience through trial and error will teach you the oven settings required to give you the results you want.

The following table is a useful guideline for cooking times and temperatures.

Conventional Oven Roasting Chart

Meat	***Oven Temp °C (°F)***	***Cooking Time***	***Internal Temp °C (°F)***
Beef	170-180 (340-355)	Rare = 20 mins per 500g plus 20 mins	60 (140)
		Medium Rare = 25 mins per 500g plus 25 mins	70 (160)
		Well Done = 30 mins per 500g plus 30 mins	80 (175)
Lamb	170-180 (340-355)	Medium = 20 mins per 500g plus 20 mins	70 (160)
		Well Done = 25 mins per 500g plus 25 mins	80 (175)
Pork	170-180 (340-355)	Medium = 20 mins per 500g plus 20 mins	70 (160)
		Well Done = 25 mins per 500g plus 25 mins	80 (175)
Chicken	170-180 (340-355)	20-25 mins per 500g plus 20-25 mins	75 (170)
Duck	170-180 (340-355)	20-25 mins per 500g plus 20-25 mins	75 (170)
Turkey	170-180 (340-355)	15 mins per 500g plus 15 mins	80 (175)

Note: a) for fan forced ovens reduce oven temperature by 10°C
b) 500 grams approximates to 1.1 pounds

Confusion over Names

As you'll see from the following list, which is by no means complete, there are a number of items used in cooking that go by multiple names. For example, a Bell pepper in the US is a Capsicum in Australia.

Allspice = Pimento = Jamaica pepper = Toute-epice
Bacon rasher = Bacon slice
Beef eye fillet = Tenderloin
Beetroot = Beet
Bicarbonate of soda = Baking soda
Biscuit (Aust/UK) = Cookie (US)
Blueberry = Bilberry = Whortleberry = Huckleberry = Hurtleberry
Bok Choy = Chinese cabbage
Borlotti beans = Saligia beans
Broad bean = Fava bean
Butternut Pumpkin = Butternut squash
Butter bean = Lima bean
Calamari = Squid
Cannelini beans = Fasiola beans
Capsicum = Sweet pepper = Bell pepper
Caster Sugar = Regular sugar that has been put through a blender
Cherry tomato = Tom Thumb tomato
Chickpeas = Garbanzos = Ceci = Chana dal
Chicken = Chook
Chook = Chicken
Coriander = Cilantro = Chinese parsley = Dhania
Corn = Sweet corn = Maize = Indian corn
Cornflour = Cornstarch
Cracked wheat = Burghul = Bulghur
Crayfish (Aust) = Lobster = Crawdad
Cumin = Jeera
Double cream = Heavy cream
Eggplant = Aubergine = Brinjal
Endive = Curly endive = Chicory = Witloof
Essence = Extract
Fasiola beans = Cannelini beans
Frosting = Icing
Fruit mince = Mincemeat
Gherkin = Pickle = Cornichon
Gooseberry = Grosella
Golden Syrup = Pale treacle
Gow chai = Garlic chives
Green bean = French bean = Haricot vert = Fine beans
Green prawn (shrimp) = Raw prawn (shrimp)
Ground corn = Maize
Guava = Guayaba = Bayabas
Hazelnut = Filbert

Icing = Frosting
Icing sugar = Confectioners sugar = Powdered sugar
Italian tomatoes = Roma tomatoes = Plum tomatoes
Jewfish = Dhufish
Ketchup = Tomato sauce (Aust) = Catsup
Kiwi fruit = Chinese gooseberry
Kumara = Sweet potato = Yam (US)
Lemon curd = Lemon butter = Lemon cheese
Lima bean = Butter bean
Lobster = Crayfish (Aust) = Crawdad
Mandarin = Satsuma (UK) = Tangerine
Marrow = Summer squash
Minced beef = Ground beef = Hamburger
Mincemeat = Fruit mince
Muesli = Granola
Okra = Bindi = Lady's fingers = Gumbo
Orange roughy = Sea perch
Paprika = Sweet paprika
Passionfruit = Maracuya = Parcha = Grenadilla = Lilikoi
Pawpaw = Papaya = Lechoza
Peanut = Groundnut = Goober pea = Monkey nut
Pepitas = Pumpkin seeds
Persimmon = Kaki = Sharon fruit
Pimento = Allspice = Jamaica pepper = Toute-epice
Plain flour = All purpose flour
Prawns = Shrimp
Profiterole = Cream puff
Quince = Japonica
Rind = Zest
Rocket = Arugula
Rockmelon = Canteloupe = Spanspek = Musk Melon
Roma tomatoes = Plum tomatoes = Italian tomatoes
Satsuma (Aust) = Red plum
Scallop = Coquille
Scone = Biscuit (US)
Self-Raising Flour = Self Rising Flour = Plain Flour (1cup)+ baking powder (2tblsp)
Shallot = Scallion = Spring onion = Green onion = Eschalot
Shelled = Shucked
Shucked = Shelled
Silver beet = Seakale beet = Swiss chard
Single cream = Light cream = Half 'n' Half
Snails = Escargot
Snow pea = Mange tout = Sugar pea
Spanish onion = Bermuda onion = Red onion
Starfruit = Carambola
Stock = Bouillon
Sultana = Seedless white raisin
Summer squash = Marrow

Sweet potato = Yam (US) = Kumara
Tamarillo = Tree tomato
Tenderloin = Beef eye fillet
Thickened cream = Heavy cream (US)
Tomato puree (Aust) = Tomato sauce (US)
Tomato sauce (Aust) = Ketchup = Catsup (US)
Turnip (Scotland) = Swede = Rutabaga
Unsalted butter = Sweet butter
White radish = Loh baak = Muli
Zucchini = Courgette = Zapallo = Baby marrow

Setting a Table

Setting a table is a little like getting out the right tools for the job, at the beginning of the job, and setting them in an easy-to-find order. In addition, a carefully set table will convey the impression that you care about the people who are going to be eating there and that you know what you're doing.

Some basic things to remember are:

- Everything should be clean. There is nothing more off-putting than food dried on knives and forks or food stains on placemats, tablecloths or serviettes (napkins).
- Make sure there is enough room at the table for your guests to sit comfortably without struggling for elbowroom.
- Have enough cutlery and crockery (preferably matching) so that you don't have to wash-up between courses.

I can remember being invited to a newly-divorced friend's place for dinner along with eight of his closest friends. He had spent hours preparing an elaborate meal, which was presented very well and it tasted great. Unfortunately, his efforts were not appreciated fully because we were so cramped at the table that we almost had to feed each other.

So, choose the type of meal and how it's going to be served based on the number of people you're going to invite. If you want to cater for the crowd scene from Ben Hur, then choose a buffet[1] style meal.

The real key is to start small. For your first few dinners invite a small group of people so you can develop a collection of recipes that work for you, and you can practice the whole process. And more importantly, you can work on your reputation as a bloke who can cook. When it comes to setting a good-looking table, keep it simple and avoid tall things in the middle of the table like a bunch of flowers or a candle. You don't want your guests to have to spend the whole meal trying to look around them when chatting with the person on the other side of the table.

1 Buffet style – food is put out on a table or kitchen counter and guests are given a plate and invited to help themselves and then to sit casually where ever they would like. One of the dangers of this style of meal is spillage in places and on things that you don't want.

Table Settings

The most basic table setting is:

a – serviette (napkin)

b – dinner fork

c – dinner plate

d – water/beer/wine glass

e – dinner knife

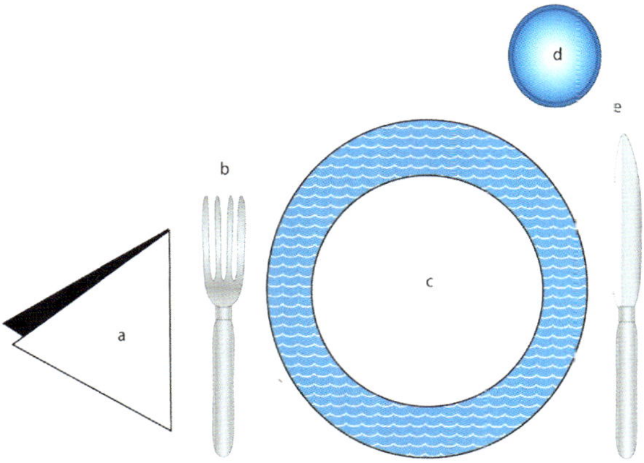

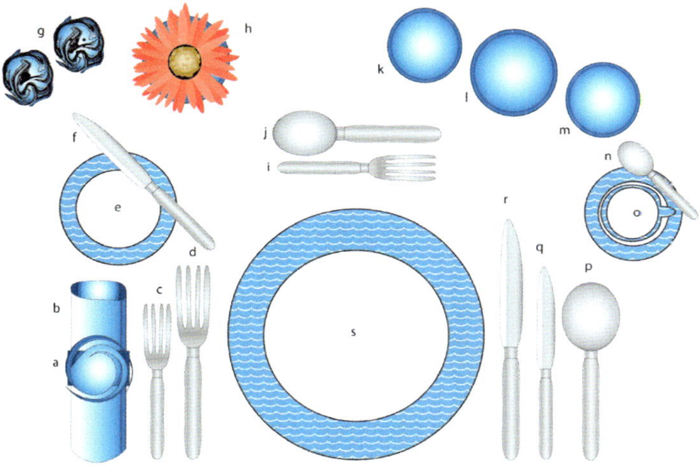

A more formal and impressive setting is:

a – serviette (napkin) ring

b – serviette (napkin)

c – salad fork

d – dinner fork

e – bread and butter plate

f – butter knife

g – salt and pepper shakers

h – small vase with flower

i – dessert fork

j – dessert spoon

k – water glass

l – red wine glass

m – white wine glass

n – teaspoon

o – cup and saucer

p – soup spoon

q – salad knife

r – dinner knife

s – dinner plate

Note that the knife blades always point towards the plate and the knives are always on the right.

The next thing to consider is whether you're going to use a tablecloth to cover the whole table or place mats for positioning at each setting. The following two photographs show how different the same place setting can look depending on which choice you make.

In choosing either place mats or a tablecloth be cautious about using white because things like red wine and beetroot do stain, though with the products available on the market today most stains can be washed out.

Knives and Forks

Stainless steel, silver and plastic are three of the choices available to you for cutlery (knives and forks). Plastic is OK for parties, picnics or outdoor dining (if you must). Indoor dining is better with metal cutlery, though whether it has plastic or metal handles is a matter of choice and your budget.

Prices will range from supermarket special cutlery through to the very expensive department store varieties. The real secret here is to get the best quality you can afford so that your cutlery will serve you well.

A good starting place is a setting for four, which can be expanded upon, as you become more adventurous, catering bigger dinner parties.

A typical place setting will include:

a – salad fork which doubles as the dessert fork

b – dinner fork

c – dinner knife

d – butter knife which doubles as a salad knife

e – soup spoon

f – dessert spoon

g – teaspoon

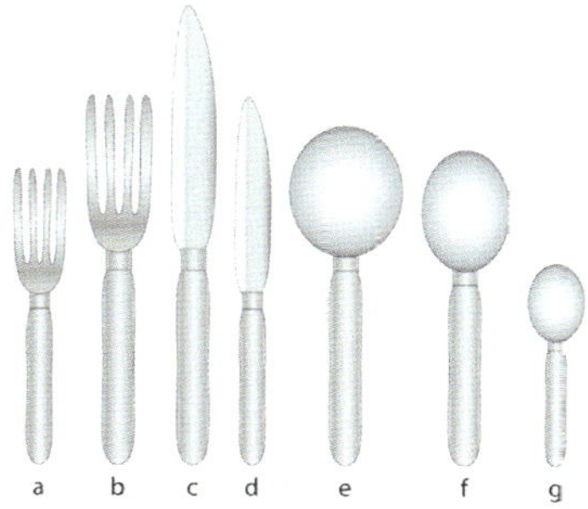

Some cutlery sets will also include serving spoons, salad servers and possibly a soup ladle. If the set you get doesn't include these items, it's a good idea to get them at the same time.

Crockery

Here again you can choose between plastic, paper or china plates, cups and bowls. As with cutlery, plastic and paper are OK for parties, picnics and outdoor dining however, indoor entertaining works best on china.

The word china covers a wide range of possibilities which include a supermarket or discount place setting for four, for less than the cost of a slab of beer (slab = two dozen cans), all the way to up-market offerings that cost as much for one place setting as a decent wide-screen TV. Let your budget be your guide.

It's a good idea to start with at least a place setting for four and choose a design that's normally available so you can expand your dinner set as the need arises.

A place setting will typically include a dinner plate, bread and butter (small) plate, soup bowl, cup and saucer. Some settings will also include a cereal bowl. A setting for four will sometimes include a sugar bowl, milk jug and salt and pepper shakers. If the set you get doesn't include the latter items, it's a good idea to get them at the same time.

Matching serving bowls and plates are also nice to have.

Serviettes (Napkins)

Paper serviettes come in a number of quality ranges, everything from no frills (which is about as soft as 120 grade sandpaper) through the high quality product from your local department store. The advantage of paper, of course, is that it's disposable at the end of the meal, whereas cloth serviettes have to be washed and ironed.

My general rule of thumb is supermarket paper serviettes for everyday use, department store quality paper serviettes for casual dining with friends and outdoor entertaining, and cloth serviettes for more formal dinner parties.

Food Preparation and Cooking Basics

This section contains some basic food preparation and cooking tips for basic foods such as eggs, rice, potatoes, vegetables, sausages etc. In the recipes section of the book you'll also find more suggestions on things to do with these basics.

Eggs

There are eggs and then there are eggs. Most recipes that use eggs don't state what size eggs are to be used, whether they're new or old, room temperature or straight from the fridge, free-range or caged, omega-modified or laid on the sunny side of the barn, however some of these things can make a difference. Well OK, not the sunny side of the barn - that just made the chicken happy. Anyway back to the eggs.

As far as the temperature of the eggs is concerned, room temperature is preferred (though not absolutely essential) for use in any recipe. For anything else, like frying, boiling or scrambling it really doesn't make any difference.

Size does matter. The larger the egg, the greater the volume in such things as scrambled eggs and meringues. I tend to buy 700g eggs (700g is the per dozen weight) because they seem to work for all my recipes and are a good size for things like poached eggs and scrambled eggs.

Eggs that are older than 2 weeks are best for hard-boiled eggs because they will peel much easier than new eggs. They're not good for separating because the membrane that holds the yolk together is not very strong and will break easily.

The best method for checking the age of an egg is to drop it gently into a pot of cold water.

If it sinks to the bottom and lies flat, it's fresh (less than 1 week old).

If it sinks to the bottom and lies at an angle, it's a middle aged egg (1 to 2 weeks old).

If it sinks to the bottom and but stands vertically, it's an old egg (more than 2 weeks old).

If it doesn't sink at all but floats insolently on the top, you should very carefully take it out of the water and dispose of it without breaking it. You'll hate yourself if it breaks because the smell will clear the kitchen, if not the house.

Scrambled

I usually allow for two eggs per person. Break the required number of eggs into a mixing bowl and beat them with a whisk or fork until a uniform colour is achieved. Add a dash of milk, or if your heart can stand it, some double cream. Stir in the milk or cream.

Put a tablespoon of olive oil in a frying pan and put it on medium heat. Scrambled eggs are best cooked slowly. When the oil is hot enough to bubble when you drop a little scrambled egg into it, pour the rest of the mixture in. Stir frequently with a wooden spoon, making sure to scrape the bottom of the pan well. Don't overcook. If you're using eggs with nothing added and you overcook them, they will be dry and hard. On the other hand, if you have added a dash of milk, the result will be a watery and unappetising mess.

While the eggs still look moist, remove them from the heat. Add ground pepper to taste and stir it through.

Serve with toast and garnish with a small sprig of fresh clean parsley placed on the top. Scrambled eggs can also be served with hot cakes, bacon, sausage, etc.

(An interesting variation is to add a little tomato sauce when beating the eggs or to use orange juice instead of the milk or cream. Your favourite cheese can also be added to the mixture once it's in the pan.)

Fried

The secret with frying eggs is not to use too much oil. There is nothing quite as off- putting as seeing eggs floating in a sea of hot fat.

Heat two tablespoons of olive oil in a frying pan until a drop of water sizzles when dropped in the oil. Break the eggs, one at a time, into the frying pan being careful not to break the yolks. As mentioned earlier, fresh eggs are best for this because the membrane around the yolk is more robust and less inclined to break.

You have some choices to make here. If you're going to serve the eggs 'sunny side up' – that's to say without turning them over – you'll need to reduce the heat and cook them more slowly so they have time to cook through, rather than have burnt bottoms and runny whites.

If you're going to turn them over, wait until the whites are mostly firm and turn them over carefully. Remove the pan from the heat and wait a minute.

My measure of a well-fried egg is one in which the yolks are runny and whites firm. It takes a bit of practice to get them that way so don't get discouraged if you don't turn out the perfect egg the first time you try.

Serve with toast and tea or coffee. Fried eggs can also be served with hot cakes, bacon, sausage, etc.

Poached

You'll find that the fresher the egg, the better for poached eggs.

Fill a saucepan to about 8cm with water and bring it to a boil. The water needs to be deep enough so the eggs are not resting on the bottom. Reduce the heat so the water is just below a simmer (no bubbles are breaking the surface). Adding a teaspoon of vinegar to the water will help hold the egg together, rather than having it spread out in the water like a demented octopus.

Break each egg into a separate glass and, when you're ready, carefully slide each one into the water. Place a lid on the saucepan and set a timer for 3 to 5 minutes depending on your taste and the temperature of the eggs. I find that when I take the eggs straight from the fridge they need to poach for 4 minutes to get firm whites and runny yolks.

Serve with toast and tea or coffee. Poached eggs can also be served with hot cakes, bacon, sausage, etc.

Preparation for Soft and Hard Boiled

Use a saucepan that's just big enough to hold the eggs snugly so they're not bounced around in the cooking process. The saucepan needs to be deep enough for water to cover the eggs.

Take each egg and using a pin or the point of a skewer, carefully make a hole in the large end of the egg being careful not to push the pin any deeper than necessary. This allows any air within the egg to escape as the temperature rises during boiling and it reduces the risk of the shell cracking.

Soft Boiled

Fill the saucepan with water and bring it to a boil.

Lower the eggs one at a time into the boiling water with a spoon. The temptation will be to drop them in using your fingers. While this is a very blokey thing to do, it endangers the eggs. They could crack when they hit the bottom.

As soon as the water begins to boil again, reduce the heat to a simmer.

Cook the eggs for 3 to 5 minutes according to your taste and the temperature of the eggs. As with poached eggs, I find that when I take the eggs straight from the fridge they take about 4½ minutes to get firm whites and runny yolks. If they're at room temperature they take about 3 minutes to get the same result. Cooking times will also vary depending on what size eggs you're using.

Serve with toast and coffee or tea. Some people like to put salt and pepper on each spoonful as they eat their soft-boiled eggs.

Hard Boiled

Fill the saucepan with cold water and place the eggs gently into the water.

Bring the water to the boil and reduce the heat to a simmer. Simmer the eggs for eight minutes.

Remove the saucepan from the stove and pour off all the water, being careful not to drop any eggs. Fill the pot with cold water and allow to stand for 15 minutes, or until the eggs are cooling to the touch.

If you don't plan to use the eggs immediately, they can be placed back into an egg carton and returned to the refrigerator. A helpful hint is to write 'hard boiled' on the outside of the egg carton because it could be quite messy if you reach for what you think is a hard boiled egg and you grab a raw one instead. I have been there and done that, and it's not so bad if you're alone at the time but, if you have company, your credibility as a cook drops down a couple of rungs, your self esteem takes a hit and you can bet that laughter will be had at your expense. So mark your egg cartons.

Sausages

Probably one of the easiest meat things to cook, and they come in a wide variety of sizes, meats and flavours. Once you have chosen what type of sausage you want, the cooking is pretty much the same. The following three ways of cooking sausages are by no means the only ways to cook them.

Preparation for each type is the same. Separate the sausages if they're connected and prick each one two or three times with a fork. This allows the internal pressures to be released as the sausages cook thereby reducing the risk of hot juices/fat being squirted on you and the appliance.

Grilled

Turn the griller on to maximum and make sure that, if the grill tray height is adjustable, it's set to about the middle.

Space the prepared sausages evenly on the grill tray and slide it in. Check the sausages every two or three minutes, turning them a quarter turn each time. This way you'll end up with a nice even golden brown.

When cooked, remove them from the griller and cover with foil for a couple of minutes, to allow the cooking to finish.

Fried

Put two or three tablespoons of olive oil in a frying pan and put it on the stove on high. When the oil bubbles if a drop of water is dropped in, reduce the heat to medium and put the prepared sausages in, spacing them evenly.

Turn the sausages frequently until they're a golden brown on all sides. Remove from the heat and place them on paper towel to drain off the excess oil. Cover with foil and allow them to stand for a couple of minutes. This will allow the cooking to finish.

Barbecued

There is a mythical belief that sausages need to have black on them if they're to be considered properly barbecued. Not true. Just because something is barbecued doesn't mean that it has to be burnt. The greater challenge, for us blokes who are out to make a reputation as an 'all right' cook, is to barbecue them to an even golden brown.

The secret is to make sure the barbecue doesn't get too hot and to turn the sausages frequently. Don't turn your back on them. Unwatched sausages will burst into flames - or at least blacken - in a heartbeat.

When cooked, stand them to the side for a couple of minutes to allow the cooking to complete and then serve.

Serving Suggestions

Sausages are very versatile and can be served for breakfast, lunch and dinner. Even as a late night snack, there is nothing better than a left over sausage and a glass of milk (or maybe beer).

Breakfast – with eggs, hot cakes, hash browns, coffee/tea.

Lunch – in a hot dog bun, with chips.

Dinner – with mashed potatoes, peas and gravy.

These are basic suggestions, a starting point; your creativity can take you to such places as sliced sausage and mushroom risotto, curried sausages and rice, etc. My suggestion is that you nail the basics first.

Bacon

Bacon can be cooked in the microwave, on the barbecue or in a frying pan. Whatever method you choose, be aware that bacon will 'spit' while it's cooking. Some basic precautions are to wear either an apron or clothing that you don't care much about. Covering the bacon with a spatter guard (see Tools of Trade) while frying helps to minimise the amount of fat that's sprayed around the kitchen.

When cooking in the microwave, place the bacon on a paper towel on a micro-safe plate and then cover with another sheet of paper towel.

The length of time that bacon is cooked is entirely individual. Some people like their bacon crispy while others like it limp.

Steak (and Chops)

One of the challenges in cooking steak is getting it cooked just right. This is particularly important when the piece of steak you're about to cook has cost you more than the cost of a slab of beer. You would not want to waste a slab of beer.

Some people like their steak still bleeding and others like it carbonised to the centre. The following table will help you cook steak to your own taste.

Doneness		Description	Temp
Black and Blue	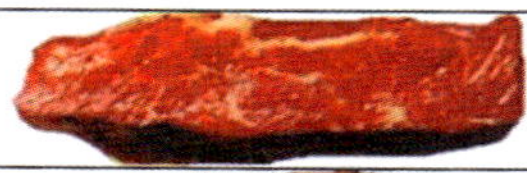	Charred black on the outside and ice-cold raw centre.	
Very Rare	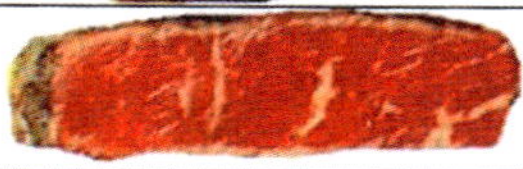	Warm in the middle. Red throughout.	55°C
Rare	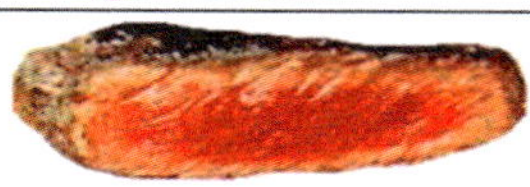	Red inside and warm in the centre. If vegetarians are offended by the sight of your rare steak, you got it right.	60°C
Medium rare	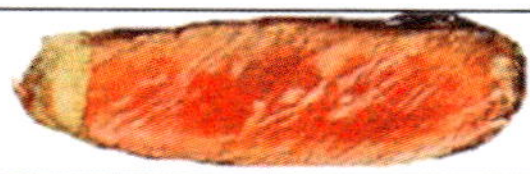	Red in the centre but completely heated. The outer rim is pink.	65°C
Medium	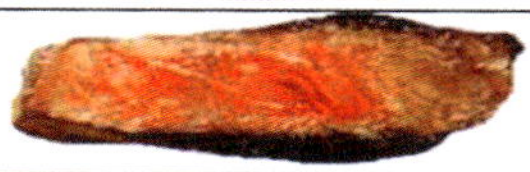	The centre is pink and most of the steak is brown.	70°C
Medium Well	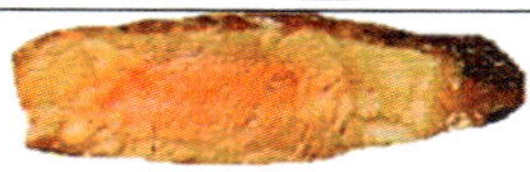	There is the slightest trace of pink in the centre.	75°C
Well		No red or pink inside. Brown throughout.	80°C

Mince Meat (Hamburger)

Mince meat or Hamburger as it's called in some parts of the world (though I am not sure why because there is no ham in it) can be prepared in a wide variety of ways, the simplest of which is patties for making hamburgers.

Hamburger Patties

At its simplest, a hamburger patty is a ball of mince meat (hamburger) that's flattened to the desired thickness and then barbecued on a hot griddle or fried in a hot frying pan until browned on both sides. Cooking on a hot griddle or pan ensures that the juices stay in. For a 2cm thick patty allow about 4 minutes per side in the cooking for medium and 3 minutes per side for medium/rare.

Serve on a hamburger bun with condiments such as tomato sauce (ketchup), mustard and mayonnaise. Sliced bread and butter pickles also add a nice touch.

The hamburger can be enhanced by adding a little bit of minced chilli (chili in the US) or some chilli powder to the raw ingredients. Make sure that you mix it through thoroughly. I usually do the mixing with my hands (see section on Hygiene), which ensures that all the ingredients are evenly spread throughout the mix. Other things that can be added to enrich the flavour are Worcestershire sauce, tomato sauce, soy sauce, mustard, sate sauce, etc. Not all of them together though. Each time you make hamburgers try adding something different and make a note of what you added and what the taste was like until you discover your 'secret recipe'.

Other ways of having mince meat

Later in the book you'll see a recipe for Spaghetti Bolognaise (Meat Sauce) and a curry dish that uses mince meat (hamburger). There is also a recipe for a non-traditional Frikadel (rissole), which my dad used to make. These are just some of the other ways to use mince meat.

Preparing Vegetables

The very first step in preparing vegetables is to wash them. This does a couple of things. First, it gets the dirt and chemicals off. It's good to get the dirt off unless you're going for that crunchy / gritty finish to your meal.

The second - and equally important - reason for this step is to wash away any unwelcome guests hiding in amongst the folds and creases. It's better for your choice of protein to remain where it's placed, rather than having it wander around the plate at will.

For salads, it's best to taste a small portion of the raw fruit or vegetable to figure out whether you like it or not. I know the first time someone suggested that I eat raw mushrooms, I looked at them as if they had grown another head. I was adventurous enough to give it a try and have been using raw mushrooms in salads ever since.

Before moving onto specific vegetables, there are some basic terms that you'll need to be familiar with in order to follow some recipes.

Slicing – is the process of cutting the item into slices of uniform thickness. The recipe will normally specify whether thick or thin slices are required. The secret is to maintain a uniform thickness in your slices because it will have an impact on the cooking time and the presentation. One of the key secrets to slicing is paying attention to what you're doing. There are a couple of reasons for this - and not the least is that you're playing with a sharp knife and the potential for blood spill is high if you get distracted. Another reason is so that uniformity of thickness can be maintained.

Dicing – is the process of cutting food up into relatively uniform cubes. The size of the cubes depends on what it's going to be used for. For example, if you were dicing carrots to include in a vegetable soup you would probably aim for cubes about 1cm (3/8in) across whereas if you were dicing watermelon for serving with ice cream you would probably aim for 3cm (1in) cubes.

Chopping – coarse, medium and fine are the three rough measures used and they refer to the size of the chunks in the finished process. For example, finely chopped onion will produce chunks about 2-3mm (1/8in), medium chunks would be 3-7mm (1/4in) and coarse would be anything bigger than that.

Julienne – refers to cutting food into thin sticks.

Mushrooms – Mushrooms come in a wide variety of sizes and types all the way from smaller than a pea to the size of a bread and butter plate. The majority of mushrooms sold in your local supermarket or green grocer are commercially grown and are safe to eat. However, some people do show an allergic reaction to them.

I would caution you against gathering mushrooms from the front lawn (or when you find them in the bush) and cooking with them or using them in a salad. While they might look similar or the same as the store bought variety, they may well kill you or your guests. This doesn't do a thing for your reputation as a chef.

The button mushroom is probably the most widely grown variety and is a really easy one to use, though the basic preparation is the same for all varieties. The first step is to wash them. The next step is to cut the end of the stem off. This is usually dry and possibly hard and won't work well in your recipe. From here, follow the recipe, which may require them whole or sliced.

Capsicum – Red, orange, yellow, green (aka Bell peppers) are not the burn-the-mouth variety of pepper. They're of the same family, but they don't contain the chemical capsaicin (which is what burns). The colour is determined by the time they're picked in their growing cycle, green being the youngest and ranging through to red. Red capsicum is sweeter.

As you can see from this photograph the capsicum has a stem and seeds that are not particularly edible and should be cut away and discarded.

If the recipe calls for them to be halved, it usually means to cut them from top to bottom and then remove the stem and seeds. Another method it to cut the top (stem end) off and remove the seeds. This method is sometimes used if they're going to be stuffed.

In salads they can be sliced or diced, or however you want to creatively cut them up.

Tomatoes – There are a wide variety of tomatoes regularly available and the choice will depend on the flavour and look that you're trying to achieve. For example, cherry tomatoes, sliced in half or crushed are a nice addition to any salad, both from the point of view of flavour and look. Vine-ripened or truss or hydroponic or whatever the description of how they were grown, the flavour should be what determines which you choose.

Tomatoes are great either raw or added to soups, stews, risottos or anywhere else you can think of adding them. However, I would draw a line at adding them to desserts.

Sliced, diced, whole and crushed are some of the ways in which they can be used. When cutting tomatoes it's imperative to use a really sharp knife or you'll simply end up making a dent in the skin and nothing else.

Onion – Onions are most commonly available in three basic varieties: brown (aka yellow), white, and red (aka Spanish). Brown onions are generally the least expensive, and have the strongest flavour. They're pretty overpowering raw, but cooking mellows their flavour nicely and brings out their sweetness. White onions are a little bit sweeter and less pungent than brown, as are red onions. Red onions, in particular, are great either raw (in salads or sandwiches, for example) or grilled.

Chopped red onions add a nice flavour and look to a salad. The only word of caution is that moderation should be observed because some people don't like to be overwhelmed by the flavour.

The secret to chopping onions is to leave the root base on until the end. This does a couple of things: it helps to keep the whole thing together as you make the initial cuts, and the onion releases less of the fumes that cause tears. These fumes, by the way, dissolve in the fluids around the eye to form a weak solution of sulphuric acid and that's why your eyes burn and you get tears when working with onions.

Back to slicing onions, the following table shows the various stages of chopping an onion.

Step 1: Cut the top off – don't cut off the root base

Peel off the dry outer skin

Step 2: Cut the onion in half from top to bottom

For coarsely chopped:

Step 3: Make a series of well-spaced parallel cuts, but don't cut through the root base, because that's what will hold it all together until you're ready to cut that section off.

Step 4: Cut at right angles to your parallel cuts. Your last cut will cut off the root stock. Make the cuts well spaced for coarse, as shown in this picture.

For finely chopped:

Step 3: Make a series of close parallel cuts, but don't cut through the root base, because that's what will hold it all together until you're ready to cut that section off.

Step 4: Cut at right angles to your parallel cuts. Your last cut will cut off the root stock. Make the cuts close for fine, as shown in this picture.

Lettuce – Pick it by colour, size and flavour. It's really a matter of taste. Iceberg lettuce is probably the least expensive and least flavoursome of them all, but it's a good basis for a garden or chef's salad. Some varieties can be quite bitter and should be used sparingly to add interest to the flavours. Cos (Romaine) lettuce is a nicely-flavoured lettuce and the type most commonly used in a Caesar Salad.

In working with any of the varieties, it's important to break the leaves from the stem and then wash and drain well before using, in order to get any dirt and unwanted guests out of the folds. Try to avoid cutting the lettuce with a knife because it will brown where the cuts have been made. It's better to break the leaves up by hand into manageable size chunks before adding them to a salad.

Celery – Here is a versatile vegetable. Every part of a bunch of celery can be used. The leafy tops can be used is soups and stews and they enhance the flavours of the other ingredients. The stalks can either be used in cooking or eaten raw, or chopped up and added to salads.

One of my kids' favourite ways of having celery was a thing called Ants on a Log and this is made by cutting the stalks into lengths, filling the hollow with peanut butter and then sprinkling with sultanas or raisins.

Carrots – A vegetable that can be eaten raw or cooked, and adds both colour and flavour to any meal. The whole vegetable is edible though the top, or greens, are seldom eaten by humans. Carrots can be eaten either peeled or with the skins on.

Potatoes – Here is another place for some confusion. Up until a few years ago, the process of buying potatoes was easy. Your choices were washed or unwashed. Pretty simple. Did you want to pay for dirt in the weight and wash it off at home, wasting your water, or did you want someone to have done that for you already?

Today your choices have broadened to include the variety of potato you need for the meal at hand. The following table represents some of the more commonly available potato varieties in your local supermarket and green grocer and will help in this decision making process.

Variety	***Cooking Quality***
Coliban 	When cooked the flesh is white. If you want a potato that will hold together in things like stews and whole boiled potato then this is not the one to choose. OK for frying.
Desiree 	Great for boiling and mashing. Holds together well when boiled or included in soups and stews. Good for salads and roasting. Not much good for frying.

Variety	***Cooking Quality***
Sebago 	This is your general purpose potato.

Preparation will depend on what you're going to do. If the plan is to do mashed potatoes then the potatoes will need to be peeled. If they're going to be eaten with the skins on it's important to brush them in order to get any residual dirt off the skin.

When peeling potatoes, you will notice that they have a tendency to go brown after being exposed to the air for a while. A way to stop this from happening is to place the peeled potatoes in a pot of cold water until you're ready for them. If you're going to roast them, be sure to dry them before you put them in the oven so that they will have a crisp outer when cooked.

Broccoli – This can be eaten cooked or raw. When buying it, look for the heads that have a purple hue. They're better. The whole head can be eaten, including the stem.

To prepare it, wash the head in cold water, for all the reasons stated earlier, and trim off any leaves. If you're going to use it for soup, cut up the main stem for cooking,. Otherwise discard it because it's a little too tough to eat. Cut the florets from the crown. If they're too big, you may need to cut them in half. (See Cream of Broccoli Soup in the recipes section. It's a rich and tasty soup.)

Cauliflower – Same as broccoli with regard to preparation with the exception that the only parts to discard are the leaves. The stem and thicker sections are quite edible and cook at about the same rate as the florets.

Other Vegetables – The majority of other vegetables only require washing and cutting up in accordance with the recipes' instructions.

Cooking Vegetables

The debate over fresh versus frozen goes on. The current view (and I agree with it) is that if you live close to the vegetable supply, and what you buy is fresh when you buy it, then there is not a lot of difference between the two. Convenience is an important factor to be considered. For example if you like peas, the only way you can buy them fresh is in the pod. Have you ever shucked peas? I have. Give me frozen peas any day. Similarly with beans, I would prefer to use frozen because they're easier to use. Furthermore, a packet of frozen anything can be put back into the freezer if you don't use all of it. Fresh vegetables, on the other hand, have a definite shelf life that should not be ignored. Have you ever seen a cucumber that has become liquid or a tomato that has grown hair? If you want to check this out, just buy fresh ones and put them in the vegetable drawer of your fridge – and wait. The message here is that when you buy fresh vegetables (and fruits) only buy what you'll eat within a few days or you'll end up throwing stuff away.

Steamed

Steaming is quite simple and the only piece of special equipment you'll need is a steamer insert for one of your saucepans. There are some fresh vegetables that are easy to steam and are quite enjoyable when done this way. The real secret is not to

overcook them and, as a guide, approximate steaming times are shown here for some of my favourites.

To steam, place a couple of centimetres of water in the bottom of the saucepan, making sure that when the steamer is inserted, it doesn't touch the water. Bring the water to a boil then reduce to a simmer. A word of caution – don't let your saucepan boil dry.

Steaming Times

Vegetable	*Minutes*
Asparagus	8-10
Beans, Green	5-15
Broccoli florets	5-6
Broccoli spears	8-15
Cabbage wedges	6-9
Carrots, whole	10-15
Carrots, slices	4-5
Cauliflower, whole	15-20
Cauliflower florets	6-10
Corn on the cob	5-7
Peas	3-5
Spinach	5-6

Wash the vegetables to be steamed and cut them up into servable size portions. Place the pieces in the steamer, put the steamer on the pan and cover with a lid. The lid should be a good fit so that steam doesn't escape.

Vegetables that have a similar steaming time can be steamed together. Some people like their vegetables more on the crisp side and others prefer them on the softer side. As you'll continue to discover, your own taste will have a bearing on how long you steam your vegetables.

Steamed vegetables can be served as they are, or with butter, or with a white sauce or cheese sauce, both of which can be found in the sauces section of this book.

Boiled

This was my mother's favourite method of cooking vegetables. They were boiled until all the colour was in the water and then they were drained and served. Unfortunately, most vegetables lose their nutrients into the water (not to mention their flavour) when they're boiled and those nutrients are then poured down the drain. The only vegetables that I tend to boil are potatoes simply because it's easier to make mashed potatoes this way. If I am serving them whole I microwave them.

Microwaved

Fast, easy and minimal mess would be the best way to describe microwaved vegetables. There are some basics when it comes to microwaving:

- Cover what you're cooking or heating (food will bubble and splatter making a mess of the inside of your microwave).
- Wipe down the inside of the microwave regularly to ensure that you're cooking what you intend to cook rather than cooking bits and pieces of the previous meals.
- Cook in short bursts. If you think something will need 1 minute, then cook it for thirty seconds – check it/stir it – and then cook for another thirty seconds. If you overcook food in the microwave there is no going back.

- Keep a careful eye on liquids because they can go from no activity to boiling over in a matter of seconds.

Most frozen vegetables will have instructions for microwaving on the packet but with fresh vegetables it will be a bit of trial and error. The key is to cook in short bursts, testing until you get the result you want.

Rice

Here are two of the many ways to prepare rice. In the recipes section of the book, you'll find Risotto, which uses a different type of rice and is another way in which rice can be prepared.

Absorption Method

INGREDIENTS:

1 cup long grain rice
1½ cups water

DIRECTIONS:

Place cold water and rice in a saucepan on high heat. Bring to the boil, stirring once or twice while coming to the boil. Reduce the heat to low, cover and simmer for ten minutes – don't stir.

Remove from the heat and allow to stand for ten minutes before serving.

Boiled

INGREDIENTS:

1 cup long grain rice
6 cups water

DIRECTIONS:

Bring water to a boil. Add the rice and stir. When the water returns to the boil, reduce heat to low. Allow to simmer for 12 to 15 minutes until rice is soft and fluffy. Stirring occasionally.

Drain and serve immediately.

Potatoes

Roasted, baked, mashed, boiled, and fried are some of the ways to cook potatoes. You'll also find a number of dishes in this book that include potatoes.

There is some confusion that's culturally based, and that's the difference between baked potatoes, roast potatoes and jacket potatoes.

Baked potatoes can be potatoes either microwaved or cooked in the oven in their jackets (washed but not peeled) or potatoes that are peeled, quartered and then baked or roasted in the oven.

Confused? I don't have a simple answer for this. In my home, we have agreed that we will refer to them as Roasted Potatoes (peeled, quartered and baked in the oven) and Baked Potatoes (scrubbed and baked whole in their skins either in the oven or the microwave).

Roasted or baked potatoes (baked pumpkin)

INGREDIENTS:

1½ kg (3lbs) Potatoes (or 1kg [2lbs] potatoes and 500g [1lb] pumpkin)
¾ cup olive oil

DIRECTIONS:

Wash and peel the potatoes (or pumpkin) and cut them into large pieces (about the size of a golf ball).

Place them in a large bowl with ¾ cup of olive oil. Stir them around until all pieces of potato are well covered with olive oil. The remaining olive oil can be poured back into the bottle for re-use, using a funnel and a piece of paper towel to act as a filter.

When the beef or pork roast is about half done, put the potatoes on the baking paper, taking care to space them evenly around it.

When the roast is done and has been removed to set (resting roast meat for 20 minutes after it is removed from the oven will enhance the texture and flavour. Just cover it with foil and set it aside.) Pour the juice out of the pan (great for making gravy), increase the oven temperature to 220°C (430°F) and return the baking pan with the potatoes for a further 20 minutes to allow them to crisp up.

Mashed Potatoes

Mashed potatoes can be a delight to eat or they can be more like trying to force down lumpy leftover wallpaper paste from last month's home renovation. I know as a child I had to endure the latter and I much prefer the former.

First, peel the potatoes and cut them into quarters, making sure to wash any dirt that might have transferred from the skins to your hands and the potatoes before you proceed to the next step.

Place them in cold water on the stove and bring the water to the boil. Reduce the heat and let them simmer for 12 to 15 minutes. To see if they're cooked, pierce with a fork. If the fork doesn't stay stuck in the potato when you take it out, the potato is cooked.

Then drain off the water.

Using a mixer on low speed, beat the potatoes until smooth. Add butter or margarine (about two tablespoons for starters – add more after tasting if necessary) and a splash of milk (add more after tasting if necessary). Mix on medium speed until a rich creamy result is achieved.

Add more butter and milk as you mix on medium speed to achieve the texture that you want. A word of caution: if you add too much milk you'll end up with something that's too thin for a fork and is more like a potato smoothie, so only add a little at a time.

Variations that can be quite effective are:

- Add a lightly beaten egg after the first beating. This will give a smoother and creamer texture.
- Add grated tasty cheese to the hot potatoes and immediately beat. The cheese will melt throughout the mixture.
- Add double cream (if your cholesterol allows it) instead of butter for a richer taste.

I always make more than I can use for the meal because left over mashed potatoes can be used in a number of other recipes such as Shepherds Pie, Cheesy Rolls, Fish Cakes, etc. or it can just be reheated in the microwave for use in another meal.

Boiled Potatoes

These are best done with their jackets (skins) left on and it's imperative that any dirt is thoroughly scrubbed off before proceeding. (Gritty potatoes have no real appeal and they certainly add nothing to a meal worth writing home to Mum about.) If you're unable to get them clean then you'll have to peel and wash them before you proceed.

Place them in cold water on the stove and bring the water to the boil. Reduce the heat and let them simmer for 12 to 15 minutes. To see if they're cooked, pierce with a fork. If the fork doesn't stay stuck in the potato when you take it out, the potato is cooked.

They can be served with the skins on. The skins are quite edible and contain some of the nutrients potatoes have to offer. There is a common myth that all the goodness is in the skin and it's exactly that, a myth.

Smothered in butter with sour cream and chives is a nice way to serve boiled potatoes.

Fried Potatoes

French Fries (not an invention of the French) or chips are a common way to have potatoes. Some words of caution: very hot oil is inflammable and doesn't take much to ignite. Whenever deep-frying anything, you should keep a constant eye on it.

As a child, I can remember a number of times when Mum or Dad got careless and we had a frying pan of hot oil go up in flames. Did you know that the smell of smoke from an oil fire takes weeks to get out of the house? Did you also know that your neighbours won't appreciate you for the adrenalin rush they get when they think your house is on fire? Especially if you live in a block of flats.

Back to the chips. First peel the potatoes and cut them into the desirable shape and size. (If in doubt go down to your local supermarket and check out the freezer cabinet for precooked versions of what you're trying to achieve.) Make sure to wash any dirt that might have transferred from the skins to your hands and the potatoes before you proceed to the next step.

Heat the oil until a sliver of chip sizzles when dropped into the oil. Carefully add the chips a few at a time. (Caution: if you dump a lot in at once there is a possibility of boil over and you could have a fire on your hands.)

When golden brown, drain well and serve. This is best done by using a slotted spoon or a pair of tongs and taking the chips out a few at a time and placing them on absorbent paper. When the oil is cool, it can be poured into a container for later re-use.

Another method for making chips is to buy the frozen ones from your supermarket and follow the instructions on the packet.

Microwaved Potatoes

Potatoes can be microwaved whole and unpeeled. First scrub them well to get off any dirt or other undesirable foreign material that would add unwanted flavours or textures to your meal. Then prick the outside liberally with a fork.

Space the potatoes evenly in the microwave and set the time for five minutes to start with. Test with a fork and, if it comes out easily, the potato is cooked. If more cooking is necessary, try doing it in one or two minute blocks until the desired result is achieved. Potatoes can be overcooked and the result is quite unpleasant.

Because the cooking will continue for two or three minutes after you take the potatoes out of the microwave, it's a good idea to let them stand for that long before serving them.

They can either be served whole or sliced in half. If sliced in half they can then be smothered in butter or sour cream. Chopped fresh chives sprinkled over the top is also a nice addition.

Pasta

Done well, pasta is great. Done poorly it takes on the characteristic of spongy tubes of wallpaper paste. The two greatest challenges with pasta are choosing which form you want to use, and cooking it just long enough.

Essentially, pasta is divided into short and long. Short pasta has descriptive names like penne, shell, macaroni, elbows, pennetta, butterflies and helix. Long pasta comes in varieties like spaghetti, linguine, fettuccine, angel hair and vermacelli. Spaghetti can be found in thin, thick and tubular.

The thing that all varieties have in common is they taste the same and they need to be cooked until they're firm but not hard.

First you need to figure out how much to cook. About 100g (3½oz) per adult is a reasonable measure.

Next fill a large pot with water. The more the better – pasta only sticks when cooked in too little water.

Bring the water to a boil.

Slowly add the pasta to the boiling water. Ideally, the water shouldn't stop boiling, but if that happens, it's ok.

Stir and stir some more! Pasta will stick together if it isn't stirred during the crucial first moments of cooking.

Start timing when the water returns to a boil. Most pastas cook in 8-12 minutes. You should regulate the heat so the pasta/water mixture doesn't foam up and over the pot sides. Lower it the tiniest bit, and everything should be under control.

Test a piece at 8 minutes. If it's cooked it will be firm all the way through with no hard bits in the middle. Keep testing every minute until your pasta gets firm but not hard.

You have now cooked perfect pasta and all you have to do is add whatever sauce you have decided to use. (See page 118 for an easy Bolognaise sauce.)

Allowing Enough Time

Apart from considering what you're going to eat, you'll need to think about how much time it will take to prepare. Allowing enough time to prepare and cook a meal will help to make your cooking adventures successful. This applies to all meals, whether complicated or simple. It particularly applies if others are going to be enjoying the fruits of your labours. It takes time to develop a reputation as good cook, and it takes no time at all (sometimes only one bad dish) to dash that reputation on the rocks.

To work out whether I have enough time, I usually work backwards from the time I want the meal to be on the table. For example, in preparing Spaghetti with Beef, Tomato and Mushroom, I use the following time line:

Sit down to eat at:	7:30pm
Allow 5 minutes to plate the food (that's the same as saying dish up) Start plating at:	7:25pm
Spaghetti takes 15 minutes (including time to drain) add *5 minutes to allow the water to come to the boil. Put water on at:	7:05pm
Sauce needs to simmer for 40 minutes. Allow 20 minutes for preparation and sautéing meat, onions, etc. Start meal preparation at:	6:05pm

*(Note: this will vary greatly from gas to electric to induction heating and over time you'll get to know this sort of thing about your own appliances.)

Recipes in this Book – How hard are they?

Each of the recipes is graded for the level of adventure upon which a bloke might want to embark. Some of the recipes are from family and friends, some are my variation on a popular theme and some are my own creation. I have tried every one of them and have listened to the feedback from family and friends in getting them 'right'. Enjoy your journey in getting them right for you.

Each recipe is graded according to this key:

easy

a little harder

a little bit harder, but not too tough

Tip: Whenever I try a new recipe, and for the next few times that I do it, I make notes as I go along. This helps me to 'get the dish right' according to my own particular style of cooking, and the peculiarities of my oven and stove.

Recipes – Soups and Salads

Entrée, appetiser, starter, first course; these are all ways used to describe the first step in a meal. This part of the meal is meant to be a relatively small portion of something that will enhance the appetite.

Though I must admit a good hearty soup and crusty bread can actually be a meal on its own.

There is some confusion over where the salad comes in the meal. In some cultures, the salad is eaten between the appetiser and the main course. In others it's eaten with the main course and in yet others it's eaten after the main course and before dessert. Salads have been included in this section because I had to put them somewhere. You choose where you want them in your meal. I would suggest that they come before dessert.

Asian Chicken Salad with Spicy Peanut Sauce

Serves 8 to10

INGREDIENTS - Salad:

1⅓ tablespoons sesame seeds
250g (9oz) snow peas
¾ cup corn kernels (fresh/frozen)
½ cup chopped celery
¼ cup chopped coriander
500g (17½oz) pasta (short bite-sized)
500g (1lb) boneless skinless chicken breasts

INGREDIENTS – Spicy Peanut Sauce:

2⅔ tablespoons soy sauce
2⅔ tablespoons unseasoned rice vinegar
¼ cup cold water
2 tablespoons sugar
¼ teaspoon salt
1½ teaspoons minced ginger root
1 teaspoon minced garlic
¼ cup ground roasted peanuts
2 tablespoons peanut oil
2 tablespoons sesame oil
2 tablespoons hot chilli oil; or to taste

Notes:

DIRECTIONS:

Toast the sesame seeds in a small, dry pan over a medium heat, stirring constantly until seeds are golden, 3-4 minutes.

Blanch fresh snow peas and corn in boiling water for 30 seconds, or thaw if they are frozen.

Cook the pasta, drain it and let it cool.

Cook the chicken in simmering water in a covered pan until it is just done, about 15 to 20 minutes. (This is also known as poaching.) Do not overcook.

To prepare the sauce, put soy sauce, rice vinegar, cold water, sugar, salt, ginger root and minced garlic in a blender and mix on high speed for 1 minute.

Add ground peanuts and mix for 1 minute more.

In a cup, combine the oils and drizzle into blender mixture while blending at low speed.

In a large bowl combine blanched or thawed corn, cooked pasta, celery, coriander and ¾ of the sauce.

Chop the chicken and arrange it, with snow peas, over the pasta mixture.

Top with the remaining sauce and toasted sesame seeds.

Serve chilled or at room temperature.

Beef, Chicken and Vegetable Soup

Serves 8 to10

INGREDIENTS:

2 medium brown onions, sliced
1 tablespoon butter or margarine
1kg (2lbs) chuck steak in one piece
1 medium chicken
1kg (2lbs) beef soup bones (from butcher)
12 cups water
2 bay leaves
8 whole black peppercorns
4 tablespoons chopped parsley
½ teaspoon thyme
2 whole cloves
1 cup diced celery
4 carrots, diced
3 brown onions, sliced
250g (9oz) peas (fresh or frozen)
Grated cheese

Notes:

DIRECTIONS:

Cook the onions in butter on medium in a large saucepan until they are translucent.

Add the beef, chicken, beef bones, water, bay leaves, whole peppercorns, parsley, thyme and cloves. Bring it all to a boil. Reduce the heat and simmer, covered, for 2-3 hours or until the meats are tender.

Stir occasionally.

Remove the meats, cool and cut into bite-size pieces. Discard the bones.

Cook the celery, carrots and peas in a little boiling water until they are barely tender. Drain.

Add the vegetables to the soup.

Heat it all thoroughly.

Sprinkle with grated cheese.

Serve with Cheesy Rolls (See Recipes – Breads and Cakes).

Broccoli and Tomato Salad

Serves 4

INGREDIENTS:

4 cups broccoli florets
2 teaspoons Dijon mustard
3 tablespoons cider vinegar
1 tablespoon extra virgin olive oil
2 teaspoons dried oregano
2 cups vine-ripened cherry tomatoes, halved
Salt and pepper to taste

Notes:

DIRECTIONS:

Steam the broccoli until it is just cooked, about 3 minutes. Set it aside to cool.

Put the mustard in a small bowl.

Gradually whisk in the vinegar, then the oil.

Mix in the oregano.

Add salt and pepper to taste.

Put the broccoli and tomatoes in a large bowl.

Add the dressing to the salad and toss to coat the vegetables.

Cover it all and refrigerate it for 1 hour.

Chicken, Mushroom and Rocket Salad

Serves 4

INGREDIENTS:

4 (about 100g [3½oz] each) flat mushrooms, thickly sliced
500g (1lb) chicken tenderloins, thickly sliced
⅓ cup olive oil plus extra for greasing
2 tablespoons balsamic vinegar
2 garlic cloves, crushed
2 tablespoons sweet chilli sauce
Salt and ground black pepper, to taste
1 bunch rocket lettuce, trimmed, washed and dried

Notes:

DIRECTIONS:

Place the mushrooms and chicken into a large bowl.

To make the marinade, combine the oil, balsamic vinegar, garlic, sweet chilli sauce and salt and pepper in a screw-top jar. Shake it all well to combine. Pour the marinade over the mushrooms and chicken and toss gently to combine.

Cover the lot with plastic wrap and refrigerate for 30 minutes.

Lightly grease a barbecue plate with oil and preheat it on medium heat.

Spoon the mushroom and chicken mixture onto the barbecue plate and cook, turning and mixing it frequently, for 6 minutes or until the chicken is cooked through

Put it in a large heatproof bowl to cool for 10 minutes.

Gently toss the rocket leaves through the mushrooms and chicken.

Serve immediately.

Chicken Sate Soup

Serves 6

INGREDIENTS:

1 medium brown onion, chopped
250g (¾lb) chicken breast, cubed
¼ teaspoon minced chilli or ⅛ teaspoon chilli powder
6 cups water
2 cups peanut butter
1 green pepper (capsicum), chopped
2 tomatoes, chopped

Notes:

DIRECTIONS:

In a large saucepan combine half the onion with the cubed chicken, chilli and water. Bring it to a boil, reduce the heat and simmer until the meat is tender.

Mix the peanut butter with a little water and cook the mixture (in a separate saucepan) stirring constantly, until it thickens and the oil collects on the surface. Add it to the chicken and water.

Add the pepper, tomatoes, and the other half of the onion and cook for 20 minutes. Stir occasionally.

Serve with Cheesy Rolls (See Recipes – Breads and Cakes).

Cream of Cauliflower or Broccoli Soup

Serves 6

INGREDIENTS:

1 whole cauliflower or 4 large heads of broccoli
1 tablespoon butter or margarine
4 tablespoons plain flour
4 cups chicken stock
Pinch of nutmeg
Salt and pepper to taste
1 cup cream
2 egg yolks, beaten
Parsley for garnish

Notes:

DIRECTIONS:

Divide the cauliflower or broccoli into small pieces, discarding the green leaves and wash it well in water.

Melt the butter or margarine in a heavy-bottomed saucepan, remove it from the heat and thoroughly stir in the flour.

Return the saucepan to the heat and cook for one minute.

Gradually stir in the stock (a little at a time or you will get lumps), add the cauliflower or broccoli and bring it to a boil.

Reduce the heat and simmer for 30 minutes.

Sieve the soup or puree in an electric blender or use a kitchen whiz, season to taste with salt and pepper and add a pinch of grated nutmeg. Add cream and egg yolks.

Reheat the soup and stir constantly until it thickens. DO NOT LET IT BOIL.

Garnish with parsley.

Serve with Cheesy Rolls (See Recipes – Breads and Cakes).

Cream of Vegetable Soup

Serves 6 to 8

INGREDIENTS:

1kg (2lbs) diced vegetables (carrots, onions, celery, leeks, cabbage, turnips, and tomatoes)
3 tablespoons butter or margarine
5 cups beef stock
Salt and pepper to taste
4 tablespoons barley
2 tablespoons cornflour
2 cups cream

Notes:

DIRECTIONS:

Sauté the vegetables in the butter in a large saucepan for 10 minutes.

Add the stock and bring it all to a boil. Add the salt and pepper.

Simmer it all for one hour.

Sieve the vegetables or puree them in an electric blender or with a kitchen whiz.

Return the mixture to the saucepan, add the barley and continue cooking.

Blend the cornflour with a little milk or water in a separate glass and slowly add it to the soup, stirring constantly.

Cook for a further 15-20 minutes.

Slowly add the cream and heat it through, but do not boil.

Serve with Cheesy Rolls (See Recipes – Breads and Cakes).

Egg Salad

Serves 4

INGREDIENTS:

8 large whole eggs
½ cup diced celery
½ cup diced sweet pickled gherkin (sweet pickles)
3 tablespoons mayonnaise
¼ teaspoon salt
Ground black pepper to taste

Notes:

DIRECTIONS:

Place 3 litres (3 quarts) of water in a medium sized pot on the stove and bring to the boil.

When the water is at a full boil place the eggs in the pot and cook at a full boil for 3 minutes. (Remember to pierce the ends.)

Remove the pot from the heat and let the eggs stand in the hot water for 12 minutes.

Remove the eggs from the water and place them in cold water.

After about 2 minutes the eggs will be easy to peel.

Slice the cooked eggs in half.

Coarsely chop the cooked egg whites. Add them to a mixing bowl with the egg yolks and the diced celery, diced pickle, mayonnaise, pepper and salt.

Fold it all together gently.

Cover and refrigerate for at least 1 hour.

Garden Salad

Serves 4

INGREDIENTS:

1 iceberg lettuce
1 red capsicum, diced
1 red onion, coarsely chopped (optional)
2 medium ripe tomatoes
2 tablespoons olive oil
Ground black pepper to taste (optional)

<u>Notes:</u>

DIRECTIONS:

Peel the leaves from a head of lettuce.

Wash them well and shake off as much water as possible.

Tear the leaves apart into bite size portions then put the torn up lettuce into a salad serving bowl.

Add the diced red capsicum and chopped red onion.

Mix it all through by hand.

Thinly slice the tomatoes.

Lay the slices in an even layer on the top.

Sprinkle the olive oil over the top.

Before serving mix all the ingredients together using salad servers or tongs in order to spread the olive oil evenly throughout the salad.

Grind cracked pepper over the top after serving if desired.

Greek Salad

Serves 8

INGREDIENTS:

6 firm ripe tomatoes, coarsely chopped
3 Lebanese cucumbers, coarsely chopped
1 red onion, sliced into rings
1 red capsicum, halved, deseeded, coarsely chopped
200g (7½oz) marinated Greek olives
220g (8oz) marinated feta cheese, coarsely chopped
1 teaspoon dried oregano
1 teaspoon salt
½ cup olive oil
¼ cup white vinegar

Notes:

DIRECTIONS:

Combine the tomato, cucumber, onion, capsicum, olives and feta cheese in a salad bowl.

Sprinkle it with oregano and salt.

Whisk together the oil and vinegar in a jug.

Sprinkle the salad with the dressing and toss it to combine all the ingredients nicely.

Serve immediately.

Make this recipe just before serving.

Hearty Chicken Salad

Serves 4
Preheat the oven to 200ºC (400ºF)

INGREDIENTS - Salad:

2 small red onions, cut into wedges
250g (9oz) vine-ripened cherry tomatoes
⅓ cup olive oil
3 cups torn ciabatta bread
2 small chicken breast fillets
1 teaspoon dried Italian herbs
200g (7½oz) mixed baby salad leaves (mescalin)
½ cup small fresh basil leaves

INGREDIENTS - Dressing:

1 small garlic clove, crushed
2 tablespoons balsamic vinegar
2 tablespoons extra virgin olive oil

<u>Notes:</u>

DIRECTIONS - Salad:

Put the onions and tomatoes in separate bowls and toss each in 2 teaspoons of olive oil.

Spread the onions on a large baking tray and bake for 20 minutes until tender.

Add the tomatoes and ciabatta to the same tray for a further 8 minutes of cooking, until bread is golden and crisp.

Toss the chicken and dried herbs in a bowl with the remaining olive oil.

Cook the chicken on a hot char grill over high heat for 4-5 minutes each side until it is just cooked through.

Tear the chicken into strips while it is still warm.

Put the salad leaves in a large bowl and add the chicken, onions, tomatoes, ciabatta and basil leaves.

Drizzle it with dressing and toss it to coat, then divide it among the plates or bowls.

DIRECTIONS - Dressing:

Combine the garlic, vinegar and extra virgin olive oil in a screw top jar and shake well.

Mango Chicken Salad

Serves 2
Preheat the oven to 200°C (400°F)

INGREDIENTS - Chicken:

4 chicken breast fillets
2 teaspoons olive oil
2 celery sticks, diced
80g (3oz) sun-dried capsicum, chopped
2 green capsicums, diced
1 small fresh red chilli, seeded and chopped
1 large mango, diced
2 tablespoons chopped mint
Mixed salad leaves
½ cup unsalted roasted almonds, chopped

INGREDIENTS - Dressing:

½ cup whole egg mayonnaise
1 teaspoon curry powder
¾ cup plain yoghurt
1 tablespoon chutney

Notes:

DIRECTIONS - Chicken:

Put the chicken fillets in a single layer in an ovenproof dish and lightly brush them with the oil.

Cover the dish with a sheet of alfoil and bake for 15-20 minutes, or until just cooked.

Cool it slightly, then cut the chicken into bite-sized pieces.

Combine the celery, capsicums and chilli in a large bowl.

Add the chicken pieces and mix it together.

Pour over enough dressing to moisten the salad.

Gently fold through the mango and the chopped mint.

Serve the salad with the salad leaves and sprinkle with the almonds.

DIRECTIONS - Dressing:

Combine all the dressing ingredients in a small bowl and mix them.

Potato Salad

Serves 6

INGREDIENTS:

6 medium potatoes, quartered and boiled (still warm)
100ml (3½oz) or so of mayonnaise
½ teaspoon hot mustard
1 strip red pepper (capsicum), chopped
3 spring onions, chopped
½ white onion, chopped
2 pickled gherkins (sweet pickles), chopped
Salt and pepper to taste

Notes:

DIRECTIONS:

Pre-boil the potatoes.

Drain them and allow them to cool, but do not cool them in the refrigerator.

Mix the mayonnaise and mustard together in a large bowl.

Add the potatoes and the rest of the ingredients. Stir it all together.

Add salt and pepper to taste.

Refrigerate it for at least 1 hour before serving.

Potato Soup

Serves 4 to 6

INGREDIENTS:

2 tablespoons butter or margarine
4 leeks, chopped, white part only
2 tablespoons minced parsley
5 medium potatoes, diced
2 cups milk, scalded
Salt and white pepper to taste
2 egg yolks
Croutons
Extra butter to serve

Notes:

DIRECTIONS:

Melt the butter or margarine in a saucepan and sauté the leeks and the parsley until lightly browned.

In a large saucepan, place the diced potatoes, sautéed leeks and parsley and enough boiling water to cover. Bring it to a boil.

Reduce the heat, cover and simmer until the potatoes are cooked.

Put the entire mixture through a sieve or puree in an electric blender or with a kitchen whiz.

Put the mixture back in the saucepan and add milk. Heat thoroughly, do not boil.

Add the salt and white pepper to taste.

Beat in the egg yolks.

Serve it with a teaspoon of butter and a few croutons in each bowl.

Serve with Cheesy Rolls (See Recipes – Breads and Cakes).

Pumpkin Soup

Serves 6 to 8

INGREDIENTS:

750g (1½lbs) butternut pumpkin
2 large white onions
250g (9oz) peeled potato
4 cups chicken stock
1 cup cream
Pepper to taste

<u>Notes:</u>

DIRECTIONS:

Peel the pumpkin and cut it into small pieces.

Put it in a large saucepan.

Chop the onions and potato. Add them, and the chicken stock to the pumpkin.

Bring it all to a boil, reduce the heat and simmer, uncovered, for 25 minutes or until all the vegetables are soft.

Either sieve the vegetables and liquid through a fine strainer or sieve or puree them using a kitchen whiz, blender or food processor.

Put everything back in the saucepan and add the cream and pepper to taste.

Bring it to a boil, reduce the heat and simmer for five minutes.

Serve with Cheesy Rolls (See Recipes – Breads and Cakes).

Roasted Potato and Mushroom Salad

Serves 4
Preheat the oven to 200°C (400°F)

INGREDIENTS:

1kg (2lbs) small new potatoes, quartered lengthways
½ cup olive oil
400g (14oz) button mushrooms, halved
¼ cup red wine vinegar
3 teaspoons whole grain mustard
Salt and ground black pepper to taste
½ cup roughly chopped fresh flat-leaf parsley

Notes:

DIRECTIONS:

Line 2 baking trays (cookie sheet) with baking paper.

Put the potatoes onto the baking trays and lightly brush with 1 tablespoon of oil.

Sprinkle moderately with salt.

Bake them for 30 minutes or until they are golden brown and crisp.

Heat 1½ tablespoons of oil in a medium frying pan over medium-high heat.

Add ½ the mushrooms.

Cook, stirring occasionally, for 3-4 minutes or until golden.

Move to a plate, cover with foil and set aside.

Repeat the process using 1½ tablespoons oil and the remaining mushrooms.

To make the dressing, combine the remaining oil, vinegar, mustard and salt and pepper in a small bowl. Whisk it well to combine all the ingredients.

Pour the dressing into the frying pan and cook it, stirring occasionally, over medium heat for 1-2 minutes or until hot.

Put the roasted potatoes and mushrooms into a large heat proof bowl.

Add the dressing and parsley and toss it all well to combine.

Spoon into a serving bowl and serve.

Split Pea and Ham Soup

Serves 6 to 8

INGREDIENTS:

2 cups dried split peas
8 cups water
1 ham hock or 500g (1lb) bacon bones
2 medium brown onions, chopped
1 medium carrot, chopped
Salt and pepper to taste
3 tablespoons chopped parsley

Notes:

DIRECTIONS:

Cover the peas with water and soak them overnight. Drain them and rinse thoroughly.

Put the peas, the 8 cups of water, the ham hock (or bacon bones), onions, and carrot in a large saucepan. Cover and cook it over a low heat for 1½ hours.

Remove the bones and sieve by pressing the vegetables and liquid through a fine strainer or sieve, or alternatively, puree by using a kitchen whiz, blender or food processor.

Remove the meat from the ham hock and chop it up coarsely. Discard the bones.

Put the chopped ham in the pureed soup.

Season the soup to taste with salt and pepper.

Re-heat and serve.

Garnish each bowl with a sprinkle of chopped parsley.

Tortured Tomato, Mini-Mushroom and Basil Salad

Serves 6 to 8

INGREDIENTS:

½ cup olive oil
2 tablespoons red wine vinegar
2 teaspoons Dijon mustard
1 teaspoon brown sugar
Salt and ground black pepper to taste
400g (14oz) small (button) mushrooms
250g (9oz) vine ripened cherry tomatoes
1 medium red capsicum
2 cups fresh basil leaves

Notes:

DIRECTIONS:

To make the dressing, place the oil, vinegar, mustard, brown sugar and salt and pepper in a screw-top jar. Shake it well to combine all the ingredients.

Wash the mushrooms and trim away the dry part of the stem.

Put the mushrooms into a large bowl. Pour ½ cup of the dressing over the mushrooms and toss it all together to combine.

Cover the bowl with plastic wrap and set it aside to marinate for 1 hour.

One at a time, crush the cherry tomatoes between your thumb and forefinger over the mushroom mixture. Take care how you do this because you can end up with more on yourself and the kitchen than in the bowl.

Cut the capsicum in half and remove the stem and seeds.

Cut it into strips and then cut the strips into small squares.

Add the capsicum and basil leaves to the mushroom mixture.

Pour the remaining dressing over the mixture, and season with salt and pepper.

Toss it gently to combine and then serve.

Notes:

Recipes – Mains

The main course, also known as the entrée in some parts of the world, is sometimes the only course depending on how much of a banquet you might be preparing.

The first time I had a group of friends over for a meal, I went for the full three-course show. From this I learned:

- Timing is very important. My dessert was ready but the soup was still cooking.
- Start out doing a one-course meal so that I could focus on getting that right.
- As I gained experience and confidence, I could move to multi-course meals.

Beef Stew (Basic)

Serves 6 to 8

INGREDIENTS:

1kg (2lbs) lean beef
¼ cup olive oil
2 large brown onions
1 large green capsicum
1 large red capsicum
2 tablespoons Italian herb mix
1½ kg (3lbs) potatoes
2 large carrots
1 cup peas (fresh or frozen)
1 bay leaf
2 cups celery greens
4 cups beef stock (See 'Jargon – Stock')
1 tablespoon cornflour

Notes:

DIRECTIONS:

Cut the beef into 2cm (¾in) cubes trimming all excess fat and gristle off in the process.

Pour the olive oil into a large saucepan and heat it over a high heat.

Add the coarsely chopped onions then reduce the heat and cook until soft and translucent.

Prepare the capsicum by removing the stem and all the seeds.

Coarsely chop the remains and add them to saucepan. Stir everything thoroughly.

Cook until the red capsicum is soft.

Add the beef and stir everything until it is well mixed and the beef has browned on all sides.

Add the Italian herb mix and stir thoroughly.

Peel and dice the potatoes into 2cm (¾in) cubes. Stir them into the mixture in saucepan.

Peel and slice the carrots and stir them into the mixture.

Add the frozen peas. Stir everything together thoroughly.

Now add the beef stock, bay leaf and celery greens (chopped) then bring mixture to a boil and reduce the heat to a gentle simmer.

Simmer covered for 45 minutes – stirring occasionally.

To thicken (if necessary) combine cornflour with water until you have a smooth paste. Add this to the saucepan, making sure you stir continuously until it is thickened.

Serve with rice or mashed potatoes (See Tips and Techniques).

Cecil's Frikadels (Rissoles)

Serves 6 to 8

INGREDIENTS:

1 large brown onion
1 large green capsicum
1 large potato
500g (1lb) lean mince beef
¼ cup plain flour
1 egg
1 teaspoon paprika
1 teaspoon Worcestershire sauce
2 tablespoons tomato sauce
Extra flour, for coating
Olive oil for frying

Notes:

DIRECTIONS:

Peel the onion and chop it up finely.

Remove the stem and all the seeds from the capsicum and chop it finely too.

Peel the potato and then use a coarse grater to shred it.

Combine the vegetables, meat, flour, egg and flavourings in a large bowl.

Mix thoroughly (this is done best with your hands). (See Hygiene)

Put the extra flour into a flat dish.

Divide the mixture into six or eight balls and coat them by rolling them in the extra flour.

Heat 2cm (¾in) of olive oil in a large frying pan. Drop a pinch of flour into the oil. When it starts to produce small bubbles, the oil is hot enough. Reduce the heat to low and carefully lower each Frikadel into the oil. Be very careful here. If the Frikadels are dropped into the oil, the chances are that you will get splashed with hot oil and it hurts.

Cook them for 20 minutes turning them at least four times to get an even golden brown on all sides.

Drain on some paper towel and serve.

Chapatti Chicken

Serves 6
Preheat the oven to 160°C (325°F)

INGREDIENTS - Chicken:

2 eggs beaten
¼ cup milk
1 cup plain flour
3 double chicken breasts
1 cup olive oil

INGREDIENTS - Chapatti Bread Lid:

1 cup plain flour
1 tablespoon olive oil
About ⅜ cup warm water (enough for a knead able dough)

Notes:

DIRECTIONS - Chicken:

Mix the eggs and milk and pour them into a flat dish.

Put the flour into another flat dish.

Halve the chicken breasts and halve them again (each double breast ends up being 4 pieces of roughly equal size).

Put them in the egg and milk mixture. Turn pieces to coat all sides with the mixture.

Take them out one at a time and roll them in the flour – making sure that each piece is well covered with flour.

Prepare a 22cm (9in) quiche dish by liberally wiping it down with olive oil.

Heat ¼ cup of the olive oil in a heavy frying pan. Put 4 pieces of coated chicken in the hot pan. Turn them over when they are golden brown on one side. When they are golden brown on the other side take them out of the pan and put them in the quiche dish.

Repeat this step until all the chicken has been browned and put, evenly spaced, in the quiche dish.

Now cover the chicken with the Chapatti Bread Lid, making sure that the pastry covers the dish completely so that no steam can escape.

Bake it for 45 minutes.

Serve with boiled potatoes and steamed vegetables or salad.

DIRECTIONS - Chapatti Bread Lid:

Place flour in a medium sized bowl, then add olive oil to the water and gradually combine with the flour until you have a soft dough.

Sprinkle plain flour onto the counter top and roll out dough until it is big enough to fit over the quiche dish.

Chicken Tarragon Risotto

Serves 2 to 3

INGREDIENTS:

¼ cup extra virgin olive oil
1 small brown onion, chopped finely
½ large red capsicum, chopped coarsely
1½ teaspoons dried tarragon
800g (1¾lbs) chicken breast, diced
1 cup chicken stock
1 packet mushroom Cup-a-Soup
2 medium ripe tomatoes, chopped coarsely
½ cup Arborio rice
½ cup cream

Notes:

DIRECTIONS:

Heat the oil in a large saucepan.

Then cook the onion and capsicum, stirring, until onions are translucent.

Add the tarragon and the chicken. Stir it all well until the chicken is completely browned.

Add the chicken stock, mushroom soup, tomatoes, and rice and bring the lot to a boil.

Reduce the heat and simmer, stirring constantly until the rice is tender. Approximately 15 minutes.

Add some boiling water if the risotto becomes too dry.

Remove pan from heat and let it stand, covered, for 10 minutes.

Return the pan to the stove on a low heat and stir in the cream until it is warmed and ready to eat.

Fish Cakes

Makes 6 to 8

INGREDIENTS:

1 cup mashed potato
1 tin of tuna or salmon (425g or 15oz)
⅛ cup plain flour
Extra plain flour
Olive oil for frying

Notes:

DIRECTIONS:

Make the mashed potatoes, or use left over mashed potatoes.

Drain the fish and put it, with potatoes and flour, in a medium sized bowl.

Combine them well.

Divide the fish and potato mixture into eight equal portions.

Roll each portion into a ball and flatten it with the palm of your hand until it is 2cm (¾in) thick.

Put extra flour into a flat dish.

Put the flattened fish cake in the extra flour and make sure that it is floured well on all sides. Take it out of the flour and set aside on some baking paper.

Heat 1cm (⅜in) of olive oil in a large frying pan. Drop a pinch of flour into the oil. When it starts to produce small bubbles the oil is hot enough. Reduce the heat to moderate to low and carefully lower each fish cake into the oil. There is an opportunity here to experience some pain. If the fish cakes are dropped into the oil, the chances are that you will get splashed with hot oil – use care whenever you are working with oil.

Cook them for 5 minutes on each side. Drain them by putting them on a clean paper towel to absorb the extra oil, and serve.

Lamb Stew

Serves 6

INGREDIENTS:

1kg (2lbs) lean lamb
4 tablespoons olive oil
2 large white onions
1 clove of garlic (Optional)
1 large green capsicum
½ teaspoon rosemary
½ teaspoon thyme
½ teaspoon sage
2 large tomatoes
1½ kg (3lbs) potatoes
1 large carrot
1 cup peas (fresh or frozen)
1 litre beef stock
1 bay leaf
1 tablespoon cornflour

Notes:

DIRECTIONS:

Cut the lamb into 2cm (¾in) cubes making sure you trim all the excess fat and gristle in the process.

Pour olive oil into a large saucepan and heat it over a high heat.

Chop the onions coarsely.

Crush the garlic (Optional) .

Add the onions and garlic to the hot oil, reduce the heat and cook them until the onions are soft and translucent.

Prepare capsicum by removing the stem and all the seeds. Coarsely chop up the remains and add it to saucepan. Stir it all thoroughly.

Add the lamb cubes and stir until it is well mixed and the lamb has browned on all sides.

Add Beef stock.

Add the rosemary, thyme and sage and stir them through the mixture thoroughly.

Coarsely slice the tomatoes and stir them into the mixture. Allow the mixture to come to a boil stirring regularly.

Peel and dice the potatoes into 2cm cubes (¾in). Stir them into the mixture in the saucepan.

Peel and slice the carrot and stir it into the mixture.

Add the frozen peas and stir in well.

Add the beef stock and bay leaf. Now bring the mixture to a boil and reduce heat to a gentle simmer.

Simmer covered for 45 minutes – stirring it occasionally.

To thicken (if necessary) combine cornflour with water until you have a smooth paste. Add this to the saucepan, stirring continuously until it is thickened.

Serve with rice or mashed potatoes (See Food Preparation and Cooking Basics).

Left-over Chicken/Beef/Lamb Risotto

Serves 4

INGREDIENTS:

1 medium white or brown onion
1 clove of garlic, crushed or finely chopped
1 large green capsicum, chopped finely
2 large red capsicums, chopped coarsely
3 large tomatoes, chopped coarsely
3 tablespoons olive oil
1 teaspoon of dried rosemary
500g (1lb) roast meat, diced
¾ cup Arborio rice
1 cup white wine

Notes:

DIRECTIONS:

Finely chop the garlic, onion and green capsicum.

Coarsely chop the tomato and red capsicum.

Dice roast meat into bite sized pieces [1cm (⅓in) cubes].

Heat oil a large saucepan.

Now cook the onion, garlic, capsicum, stirring, until the onions are translucent.

Add the tomatoes, rosemary

Add diced meat.

Add the rice and wine and bring the mixture to a boil.

Reduce heat and simmer, stirring constantly until the rice is tender, approximately 15 minutes.

Add some boiling water if the risotto becomes too dry.

Remove the pan from heat and let it stand, covered, for 10 minutes.

Lily's Macaroni Cheese

Serves 8
Preheat the oven to 180°C (355°F)

INGREDIENTS:

500g (17½oz) macaroni

⅓ cup olive oil
½ cup plain flour
¼ teaspoon hot English mustard
Pinch cayenne pepper
6 cups milk
400g (14oz) tasty cheese, grated for sauce

250g (9oz) tasty cheese, grated for topping

<u>Notes:</u>

DIRECTIONS - Macaroni:

In a large saucepan, bring 5 litres (5 quarts) of water to a boil and add the macaroni.

When it returns to the boil, reduce the heat and simmer it for 10 to 12 minutes – stirring occasionally – until the macaroni is tender throughout.

While the macaroni is cooking, prepare the cheese sauce.

Drain the macaroni in a large colander and return it to the saucepan.

Add the cheese sauce (see directions below) to the macaroni and stir it thoroughly.

Wipe down a large casserole dish with olive oil (a clean paper towel works well here) and pour the macaroni and sauce into the dish.

Spread the 250g of grated cheese evenly over the top of the casserole and bake it (uncovered) in the preheated oven until the top is golden brown (45 minutes to an hour).

Take the casserole out of the oven and allow it to stand for ten minutes before serving.

DIRECTIONS - Cheese Sauce:

In a medium saucepan, heat the olive oil.

When the oil is hot, reduce heat to low, add the flour and stir vigorously.

Add the mustard and cayenne pepper and stir in well.

Add the milk a little at a time, stirring continuously to get a smooth paste. If the milk is added too quickly the result will be lumpy. Not a good look.

When all the milk is added, increase the heat and continue to stir until the liquid is steaming.

Add the 400g of grated cheese, a handful at a time, stirring each time until the cheese has completely melted. When all of the 400g has been added and has melted, take the sauce off the heat.

Marion's Fish Bake

Serves 2
Preheat the oven to 180°C (355°F)

INGREDIENTS:

2 eggs
½ cup flour
750g (1½lbs) fish fillets

3 tablespoons butter
3 tablespoons flour
1 can cream of mushroom soup
½ cup dry white wine
2 tablespoons Parmesan cheese
2 teaspoons parsley flakes

Notes:

DIRECTIONS:

Coating the fish:

Lightly beat two eggs and pour them into a flat dish

Place ½ cup flour in another flat dish

Take each fish fillet and coat it evenly in egg and then roll it in the flour and set it aside on a cutting board

Prepare a small casserole dish by wiping it down with butter or margarine.

Put the fillets into the casserole dish, spacing them evenly on the bottom.

Melt the butter in a saucepan and stir the flour into it.

Add the soup (undiluted) and the wine.

Cook the mixture, stirring constantly until it boils and thickens. Add the cheese and the parsley.

Mix thoroughly and then pour over the fish.

Cook covered for about 35 minutes.

Serve over rice with green vegetables.

Mushroom, Spinach and Lemon Risotto

Serves 4

INGREDIENTS:

3 tablespoons olive oil
2 medium brown onions, chopped finely
2 cloves garlic, crushed
1 tablespoon finely grated lemon zest
300g (11oz) button mushrooms, halved
2 cups Arborio rice
6 cups chicken stock
1 cup dry white wine
300g (11oz) baby spinach leaves
2 tablespoons fresh lemon thyme, coarsely chopped

Notes:

DIRECTIONS:
Heat the oil in a large saucepan.

Cook the onion, garlic, zest and mushrooms together, stirring until mushrooms are browned.

Add the rice, stock and wine, and bring to a boil.

Reduce the heat to a simmer. Simmer, covered, for 15 minutes, stirring midway through the cooking.

Remove the pan from heat and let it stand, covered, for 10 minutes.

Gently stir in the spinach and lemon thyme.

Beef Stew with Red Wine and Mushrooms

Serves 6 to 8

INGREDIENTS:

1kg (2lbs) lean beef (pretty much any cheap cut of beef will do)
¼ cup olive oil
2 large brown onions, coarsely chopped
1 clove garlic, crushed
1 large green capsicum
1 litre of beef stock
1 teaspoon paprika
2 large tomatoes
1½ kgs (3lbs) potatoes
2 large carrots
1 cup peas (fresh or frozen)
1kg (2lbs) mushrooms
1 bottle cabernet sauvignon wine (We're talking VERY cheap wine here)
1 bay leaf
1 tablespoon cornflour

Notes:

DIRECTIONS:

Cut the beef into 2cm (¾in) cubes, being sure to trim all excess fat and gristle in the process.

Pour the olive oil into a large saucepan and heat it over a high heat. Add coarsely chopped onions and crushed garlic to the oil. Reduce the heat and cook until the onion is soft and translucent.

Prepare the capsicum by removing the stem and all the seeds. Coarsely chop up the remains and add them to the saucepan. Stir the mixture thoroughly.

Add the beef cubes and stir until well mixed and the beef has browned on all sides.

Add the beef stock and paprika and stir thoroughly.

Coarsely slice tomatoes and stir into mixture, then allow it to come to a boil, stirring regularly.

Peel and dice the potatoes into 2cm (¾in) cubes. Stir them into the mixture in saucepan.

Peel and slice the carrots and stir them into the mixture.

Add frozen peas and stir them in well.

Slice mushrooms and stir them into the mixture.

Add the wine and bay leaf and bring the mixture to the boil. Reduce the heat to a gentle simmer.

Simmer covered for 45 minutes – stirring occasionally.

To thicken (if necessary) combine cornflour with a little water until you get a smooth paste. Add this to the saucepan stirring continuously until thickened.

Serve with rice or mashed potatoes (See Food Preparation and Cooking Basics).

Rice with Spinach and Feta Cheese

Serves 6

INGREDIENTS:

3 tablespoons olive oil
1 large onion, chopped coarsely
2 large garlic cloves, crushed
1¼ cups uncooked long-grain rice
2 cups chicken stock
¼ cup dry white wine
420g (15oz) fresh (English Spinach) baby spinach leaves (rinse well and remove any large stems), very coarsely chopped
2 medium tomatoes, chopped
1 cup crumbled feta cheese (or blue cheese)
Pepper, to taste

<u>Notes:</u>

DIRECTIONS:

Pour the olive oil into a large saucepan and heat it over a high heat.

Add coarsely chopped onion and crushed garlic. Reduce the heat and cook them until the onion is soft and translucent.

Add the rice and stir it all for about 2 minutes or until the rice is translucent.

Now carefully add the chicken stock and wine.

Stir the mixture thoroughly and bring it to the boil.

Reduce the heat to low, cover and cook it for about 15 minutes or until the rice is almost tender.

Now stir in the spinach, cover and cook for another 8 minutes, or until all the liquid has been absorbed.

Chop the tomatoes and crumble the cheese

Mix in the tomatoes and cheese and season with pepper.

Serve it immediately.

Rita's Roast

Serves 4
Preheat the oven to 180°C (355°F)

INGREDIENTS:

2 kgs (4½lbs) beef rump roast
Paprika, salt and pepper for rubbing
3 tablespoons olive oil
1 small onion
1 to 2 bay leaves
8 to 10 whole black peppercorns
8 medium potatoes, peeled and quartered

Notes:

DIRECTIONS:

Grease the bottom of a roasting pan.

Shake paprika, salt and pepper on each side of the roast and rub it around with your fingers. (See Hygiene)

Put oil into a frying pan and heat it.

When oil is hot, put the roast into the pan and brown both sides of it to seal in the juices, and then put it in the roasting pan.

Quarter the onion and put it on top of the roast.

Add a bay leaf or two on top, along with 8 to 10 whole black peppercorns.

When the roast is about half done, put the potatoes in the pan spread evenly around the piece of meat.

Turn every so often.

If it gets dry before it is done, add a little water to the pan.

Cook until done to your taste.

Cooking Times:

Medium Rare: 1 hour
Medium: 1 hour 15 minutes
Well Done: 1 hour 30 minutes

When it is done let it stand covered for ten minutes to allow the meat to set.

Carve and serve.

Roast Lamb Dinner

Serves 6 to 8 (plus left over lamb for risotto or curry)
Preheat the oven to 180°C (355°F)

INGREDIENTS:

1 leg of lamb or lamb forequarter
1 tablespoon olive oil

In our house, the vegetables served with the 'Sunday Roast' are roast potatoes, roast pumpkin and peas, all covered with lashings of gravy.

It is important that the meat be completely thawed before roasting.

Notes:

DIRECTIONS:

Rub the lamb all over with the oil.

Place the lamb, fatty side uppermost, on baking paper in a baking pan. Add potatoes and pumpkin. (See Roast Potatoes p. 40).

Roast, uncovered, for the time required.

Rotate the pan in the oven every 30 minutes and turn the potatoes and pumpkin over at the same time.

When the lamb is done the way you like it, transfer it to a serving plate and cover it with foil. Then let it sit in a warm place for 10 - 20 minutes before carving.

Cooking Times:

Medium Rare: 25 minutes per 500g (1lb)
Medium: 30 minutes per 500g (1lb)
Well Done: 35 minutes per 500g (1lb)

Save the pan juices for Lamb Gravy.

Serve with:

Lamb gravy (See Sauces - Meat Gravy).

Roast potatoes (See Food Preparation and Cooking Basics).

Peas or mixed vegetables (See Food Preparation and Cooking Basics, p. 40).

Savoury Beef/Chicken/Lamb Curry

Serves 6

INGREDIENTS:

700g (1½lbs) roast meat
¼ cup olive oil
1 clove garlic, crushed
3 large brown onions, coarsely chopped
2 large red capsicums
2 large green capsicums
2 sticks celery
2 tablespoons curry powder
5 medium zucchini
1 cup frozen peas
3 large vine ripened tomatoes, chopped
1 cup boiling water
1 cup long grain rice

<u>Notes:</u>

DIRECTIONS:

Chop the roasted meat into 1cm (⅜in) cubes.

Pour the olive oil into a large saucepan and heat it over a high heat. Add coarsely chopped onions and crushed garlic to the hot oil. Reduce the heat and cook until the onions are soft and translucent.

Prepare the capsicum by removing the stem and all the seeds. Coarsely chop the remains and add them to the saucepan. Stir carefully.

Prepare celery by chopping it into 1cm slices and add them to the saucepan with the capsicum. Stir thoroughly and cook it all until red capsicum is soft.

Add the meat cubes to the saucepan. Stir them in well.

Add the curry powder and stir it in thoroughly. Allow the mixture to simmer for 3 minutes.

Slice off the top and bottom of the zucchini and cut into 1cm thick slices. Add them to the saucepan.

Add the frozen peas and chopped tomatoes and stir them in well.

Add the boiling water and bring mixture to the boil then reduce the heat to a gentle simmer.

Simmer covered for 25 minutes – stirring occasionally.

Serve over cooked rice (See Food Preparation and Cooking Basics).

Spaghetti Bolognaise

Serves 8

INGREDIENTS:

1 tablespoon olive oil
2 large onions, chopped
1 large clove garlic, crushed
1 kg (2lbs) beef mince (hamburger)
2 cups beef stock
1 cup red wine
3 x 400g (14oz) cans crushed tomatoes
Salt and pepper to taste
500g (17½oz) spaghetti
Grated Parmesan

Notes:

DIRECTIONS:

Heat the olive oil in a saucepan over a medium heat, then add in the chopped onions and crushed garlic.

Cook for 4-5 minutes.

Increase heat to high.

Gradually add the beef mince and cook until well browned.

Add beef stock, red wine and crushed tomatoes.

Bring it all to the boil then reduce the heat to low and simmer, partially covered, for 1½ hours, stirring occasionally.

Season with salt and pepper.

Cook spaghetti in boiling water, until firm but not hard in the centre (See Pasta, p.42).

Drain.

Serve half the bolognaise with the pasta and freeze the remaining sauce for later.
Sprinkle with grated Parmesan and serve.

Sweet Lamb Curry

Serves 6

INGREDIENTS:

¼ cup olive oil
2 large brown onions, coarsely chopped
2 large red capsicums
1kg (2lbs) lean lamb mince
1 tablespoon curry powder
750g (1½lbs) potatoes
2 apples (any of the sweeter varieties)
1 cup frozen peas
½ cup sultanas
½ cup raisins
1 cup boiling water
1 cup long grain rice (cooked)

Notes:

DIRECTIONS:

Pour the olive oil into a large saucepan and heat it over a high heat. Add coarsely chopped onions and reduce the heat, then cook the onions until they are soft and translucent.

Prepare the capsicum by removing the stem and all the seeds. Coarsely chop the remains and add them to the saucepan. Stir thoroughly.

Cook the mixture until the red capsicum is soft.

Add the lamb mince and stir it until it is well mixed and lamb has browned.

Add the curry powder and stir the mixture together. Allow it to simmer for 3 minutes.

Peel and dice the potatoes into 1cm (⅜in) cubes. Stir them into the mixture in saucepan.

Now peel and roughly chop the apples and stir into the mixture.

Add the frozen peas, and the sultanas and raisins and stir them in well.

Add the boiling water. Bring the mixture to a boil and reduce the heat to a gentle simmer.

Simmer covered for 25 minutes – stirring occasionally.

Serve over cooked rice (See Food Preparation and Cooking Basics).

Tomato and Garlic Beef Stew

Serves 6

INGREDIENTS:

1kg (2lbs) lean beef
¼ cup olive oil
2 large brown onion, coarsely chopped
2 cloves garlic, crushed
1 large green capsicum
2 large red capsicums
2 tablespoons Italian herb mix
1kg (2lbs) tomatoes
1½ kg (3lbs) potatoes
2 large carrots
1 cup peas (fresh or frozen)
4 cups beef stock
1 bay leaf
Celery greens
1 tablespoon cornflour

Notes:

DIRECTIONS:

Cut the beef into 2cm (¾in) cubes. Trim all excess fat and gristle off the meat.

Pour the olive oil into a large saucepan and heat it over a high heat. Add coarsely chopped onions and crushed garlic to the hot oil. Reduce the heat and cook until the onions are soft and translucent.

Prepare the capsicum by removing the stem and all the seeds. Coarsely chop up the remains and add them to saucepan. Stir it all together thoroughly.

Add the beef cubes and stir them until the mixture is well mixed and the beef has browned on all sides.

Now add in Italian herb mix and stir it thoroughly.

Coarsely slice the tomatoes and stir them into the mixture. Allow the mixture to come to a boil stirring it regularly.

Peel and dice the potatoes into 2cm (¾in) cubes and stir them into the mixture.

Peel and slice the carrots and stir them into the mixture.

Add the peas and stir them in well.

Add the stock, bay leaf and celery greens (chopped). Bring the mixture to a boil and reduce the heat to a gentle simmer.

Simmer covered for 45 minutes – stirring occasionally.

To thicken (if necessary) combine cornflour with a little water until you have a smooth paste. Add this to the saucepan, stirring continuously until thickened.

Serve with rice or mashed potatoes (See Food Preparation and Cooking Basics).

Notes:

Recipes – Gravy and Sauce

A yummy gravy or sauce can turn the mundane into a taste treat.

Easy Cheese Sauce

Makes 1 cup

INGREDIENTS:

1 cup milk
40g (1½oz) butter softened
2 tablespoons plain flour
Pinch of cayenne pepper
Pinch of dry mustard
250g (9oz) tasty cheese grated

This sauce goes really well over vegetables especially broccoli.

Notes:

DIRECTIONS:

Bring the milk to a simmer in a 1 litre (1 quart) saucepan over moderate heat.

Meanwhile, in a small bowl, blend the butter, mustard, cayenne pepper and flour together with a spoon to form a smooth paste.

Using a wire whisk, vigorously beat the butter-flour mixture, 1 rounded teaspoonful at a time, into the hot milk.

Cook, stirring constantly, over moderate heat for 2 to 3 minutes, or until the sauce is smooth and thick.

Add cheese a little at a time until it is completely melted.

Do not boil as it will go quite odd.

Easy White Sauce

Makes 1 cup

INGREDIENTS:

1 cup milk
40g (1½oz) butter or margarine, softened
2 tablespoons plain flour
¼ teaspoon salt
Pinch black pepper

Try this easy method of making white sauce without lumps. Use it in casseroles, over vegetables and for making creamed soups or creamed chicken or tuna.

Notes:

DIRECTIONS:

Bring the milk to a simmer in a 1 litre (1 quart) saucepan over moderate heat.

Meanwhile, in a small bowl, blend the butter and flour together with a spoon to form a smooth paste.

Using a wire whisk, vigorously beat the butter-flour mixture, 1 rounded teaspoonful at a time, into the hot milk.

Cook, stirring constantly, over moderate heat for 2 to 3 minutes, or until the sauce is smooth and thick.

Season with the salt and pepper.

Meat Gravy

Makes 3 cups

INGREDIENTS:

Juice/dripping from roasting pan
3 tablespoons plain flour
3 cups boiling water

Notes:

DIRECTIONS:

When the roast is cooked, pour all of the juices into a small saucepan.

Be sure to scrape as much of the brown residue from the baking paper and pan as possible into the saucepan. This will add both colour and flavour to your gravy.

Put the saucepan over a high heat and bring the liquid to a boil.

Reduce the heat and allow contents to simmer for three to five minutes.

Remove the pan from the heat and add the flour immediately. Stir continuously until the flour is fully combined.

Put the pan back on low heat for three minutes – stir continuously.

Add the boiling water, a small amount at a time – stirring continuously to avoid lumps.

Note: Depending on the consistency of the gravy that you want, you may not need all the water.

When you have got the result you want, remove the pan from heat and cover it so it keeps warm, ready for serving.

Notes:

Recipes – Breads, Cakes, Biscuits, Desserts

…and sometimes I skip the first and second courses and go straight to dessert.

This section has a variety of things, from Chapatti Bread and Cheesy Rolls (to accompany soups and main meals), to Blender Mousse and Lemon Self-Saucing Pudding (as a nice finish to a meal).

You will also find Cat's Tongues and other such sweet fare for other occasions.

Anzac Biscuits

Makes 26
Preheat the oven to 180°C (355°F)

INGREDIENTS:

1 cup plain flour
⅔ cup sugar
1 cup rolled oats
1 cup desiccated coconut
125g (4½oz) unsalted butter
¼ cup golden syrup
½ teaspoon bicarbonate of soda
1 tablespoon boiling water

Variation

Use treacle or honey in place of the golden syrup.

Storage time:

Store biscuits in an airtight container for up to three days. May be frozen.

Hint:

Instant or 1-minute oats are quite suitable for this recipe.

Notes:

DIRECTIONS:

Line a baking tray (cookie sheet) with baking paper.

Sift flour and sugar into large mixing bowl. Add oats and coconut; make a well in the centre.

Combine butter and golden syrup in small pan. Stir over low heat until butter has melted and mixture is smooth; remove from heat.

Dissolve bicarbonate of soda in water; immediately mix it into the butter mixture. It will foam up instantly.

Pour butter mixture into the well in the dry ingredients. Using a wooden spoon, stir until well combined.

Drop one rounded tablespoon of mixture at a time onto prepared tray, allowing room for spreading. Flatten gently with a fork.

Bake for 18 minutes or until golden brown. To achieve an all round crispness and a soft/ chewy centre use two baking trays positioned in the middle and upper halves of the oven for baking. Switch them around half way through their time.

Remove from oven; allow to cool on trays for five minutes, and then transfer biscuits to a wire rack to cool.

.

Blender Mousse

Serves 6

INGREDIENTS:

4 eggs
1 block (200g or 7oz) semisweet chocolate or 1 packet (200g or 7oz) choc-bits
5 tablespoons boiling water or coffee
½ teaspoon vanilla essence or 2 tablespoons rum

Chocolate mousse (pronounced Moose) is a creamy, decadent dessert with a rich, thick texture and robust flavour. This chocolate mousse requires at least 50 minutes chilling time, but you can prepare it as much as a day ahead and refrigerate it. The mousse can be topped with cream whipped just before serving or with thickened whipped cream.

Notes:

DIRECTIONS:

Separate the eggs, placing the whites in a small mixing bowl and the yolks in a cup. Beat the egg whites until stiff but not dry. Put aside. (See 'Tips & techniques - Working with Egg Whites, p. 14)

Break the chocolate block into small pieces and put them into the jar of an electric blender. Switch on and off to break up the pieces. Add the boiling water or coffee, and blend until smooth.

Add the egg yolks and vanilla. Blend 1 minute, or until thoroughly mixed. Pour the chocolate mixture slowly over the egg whites, and fold in gently with a metal spoon until no white shows. Spoon into individual dessert dishes or a one-litre serving dish.

Refrigerate 50 minutes, or until firm and well chilled.

Butter Cream Icing

Makes 2½ cups
Enough to cover a 20cm (8in) or 23cm (9in) round cake or 12 cupcakes. To fill and ice a two-layer cake, double the recipe.

INGREDIENTS:

60g (2oz) butter, softened
2 cups icing sugar, sifted
1½ to 2 tablespoons milk
½ teaspoon vanilla essence

Variations:

1. To make chocolate icing add two tablespoons cocoa into the sifted icing sugar.

2. Use orange essence, lemon essence or almond essence in place of the vanilla essence to get a different flavour.

Notes:

DIRECTIONS:

In a mixing bowl, cream the butter until light and fluffy.

Gradually beat in about half the sugar until well blended.

Beat in the milk and vanilla.

Gradually beat in the remaining sugar. If necessary, add a few drops more milk to make the icing more spreadable.

Cat's Tongues

Makes 40
Preheat the oven to 180°C (355°F)

INGREDIENTS:

80g (3oz) unsalted butter, chopped
⅔ cup icing sugar, sifted
2 egg whites
2 tablespoons caster sugar
¾ cup plain flour

Variation:

Add half teaspoon finely grated orange or lemon zest to mixture if desired.

Storage:

Store biscuits in airtight container.

Notes:

DIRECTIONS:

Line a baking tray (cookie sheet) with baking paper.

Beat butter and icing sugar in small bowl until light and creamy.

Transfer mixture to large mixing bowl.

Place egg whites in small mixing bowl. Using electric beaters, beat egg whites until firm peaks form.

Add caster sugar gradually, beating until mixture is thick and glossy and all sugar is dissolved.

Using a metal spoon, fold egg mixture into butter mixture; add sifted flour.

Fold flour in quickly and lightly. Do not over mix.

Spoon mixture into a piping bag fitted with a 1cm-wide plain piping nozzle; pipe mixture into 8cm (3in) lengths onto prepared tray, allowing room for spreading.

Bake for 10 minutes or until lightly golden.

Remove from oven and let stand on tray for 1 minute before transferring to wire rack to cool.

Dust with icing sugar before serving. Serve with ice-cream.

Chapatti Bread

Makes 10 to 12

INGREDIENTS:

2 cups plain flour
1 tablespoon olive oil
About ¾ cup warm water (enough for a kneadable dough)

Notes:

DIRECTIONS:

Mix flour, olive oil and enough water to make a soft but not sticky dough.

Knead the dough, cover, and leave aside for at least half an hour or, ideally, up to 2 hours.

After about 1 hour (or right before rolling out), punch the dough and knead again without any more water.

Make 10-12 4cm (1½in) balls. Dip each one into dry plain flour, and roll out into thin, 15cm (6in) circles.

Place a flat, ungreased griddle on the stove at medium-high heat. When hot, place a rolled-out chapatti "right side" down on the griddle. (The "right side" is the one facing up when you roll it.)

When bubbles are visible, turn over and cook until tiny brown spots appear on the side facing the griddle.

If you have a gas stove, hold the chapatti gently with a pair of tongs, and place it directly over the burner flame for a few seconds, until the chapatti puffs up.

Turn and repeat on the other side.

If you have an electric stove, keep the chapatti on the griddle. With a wadded up paper towel to protect your fingers, press gently all over the chapatti. Flip the chapatti and press gently over the other side.

This procedure should make the chapatti puff up. (If you press too hard, the chapatti will become too crunchy.)

Remove the chapatti from the heat, and butter on the 'right side'.

Cheesy Rolls

Makes 10
Preheat the oven to 230°C (450°F)

INGREDIENTS:

150g (5½oz) peeled potatoes, chopped
2 cups plain flour
4 teaspoons baking powder
Pinch of salt
125g (4½oz) finely grated extra tasty cheddar
½ cup milk

Notes:

DIRECTIONS:

Put the potatoes into a medium size saucepan, cover with warm water and boil until tender — about 10 minutes.

Drain and mash thoroughly. Allow to cool slightly.

Meanwhile, line a baking tray (cookie sheet) with baking paper.

Sieve the flour, baking powder and salt into a mixing bowl.

Chop the potatoes into 2cm (¾in) cubes

Add the cheese and the potatoes and quickly blend with your fingers. (See Hygiene)

Add the milk and mix to make a soft but dry dough.

Break the dough into 10 pieces and swiftly shape into balls.

Place them on the baking tray — evenly spaced.

Bake for about 15 minutes until golden brown.

Eat while still hot with lashings of butter.

Chocolate Chip Cookies (Traditional USA)

Makes about 48
Preheat the oven to 190°C (375°F)

INGREDIENTS:

¼ cup butter (at room temperature)
¼ cup sugar
½ cup brown sugar
1 egg
1 cup plain flour
½ teaspoon bicarbonate of soda
¾ cup chocolate chips or chopped chocolate drops
1 cup chopped walnuts
Zest of 1 orange, grated

Notes:

DIRECTIONS:

Line baking tray (cookie sheet) with baking paper.

Cream butter, sugar and brown sugar together until light and fluffy.

Add egg and beat thoroughly.

Sift flour and bicarbonate of soda into mixture and beat.

Stir in chocolate chips or pieces, nuts, and orange zest.

Drop teaspoonfuls of mixture on baking tray, (cookie sheet), allow room for spreading, and bake for about 10 minutes until golden brown.

Cool and serve.

Coconut Macaroons

Makes 60
Preheat the oven to 160°C (325°F)

INGREDIENTS:

3 egg whites
1¼ cups caster sugar
½ teaspoon coconut essence
1 teaspoon grated lemon zest
2 tablespoons cornflour, sifted
3 cups desiccated coconut
125g (4½oz) dark chocolate melts (squares), melted

Notes:

DIRECTIONS:

Line two baking trays (cookie sheets) with baking paper.

Place egg whites in a small, dry mixing bowl. Using electric beaters, beat egg whites until firm peaks form.

Add sugar gradually, beating constantly until mixture is thick and glossy and all the sugar is dissolved.

Add essence and zest; beat until just combined.

Transfer mixture to large mixing bowl. Add cornflour and coconut.

Using a metal spoon, stir until just combined.

Drop 2 level teaspoons of mixture per biscuit, onto prepared trays about 3cm apart.

Bake on top shelf 15-20 minutes or until golden.

Cool macaroons on trays.

Dip half of each biscuit (cookie) into melted chocolate; allow to set before serving.

Cornflake Biscuits (Cookies)

Makes 30
Preheat the oven to 180°C (355°F)

INGREDIENTS:

125g (4½oz) unsalted butter
¾ cup sugar
2 eggs, lightly beaten
1 teaspoon vanilla essence
2 tablespoons currants
1½ cups desiccated coconut
½ teaspoon bicarbonate of soda
½ teaspoon baking powder
2 cups plain flour
3 cups cornflakes, lightly crushed

Notes:

DIRECTIONS:

Line a baking tray (cookie sheet) with baking paper.

Using electric beaters, beat butter and sugar in small mixing bowl until light and creamy.

Add eggs gradually, beating thoroughly after each addition.

Add essence; beat until combined.

Transfer mixture to a large mixing bowl; add currants and coconut.

Sift bicarbonate of soda, baking powder and flour.

Using a metal spoon, fold into the mixture, and stir until ingredients are just combined and the mixture is almost smooth.

Drop level tablespoons of mixture onto the cornflakes and roll into balls.

Arrange on prepared tray, allowing room for spreading.

Bake for 20 minutes or until crisp and golden.

Transfer biscuits (cookies) to wire rack to cool.

Store in airtight container.

Cream Cheese Icing (Frosting)

Makes 2½ cups
Enough to cover a 20cm (8in) or 23cm (9in) round cake or 12 cupcakes. To fill and ice a two-layer cake, double the recipe.

INGREDIENTS:

100g (3½oz) cream cheese, softened
40g (1½oz) butter or margarine, softened
½ teaspoon vanilla essence
2 cups icing sugar, sifted

Variations:

1. Chocolate Icing – Blend 2 melted squares (60g or 2oz) unsweetened chocolate into the butter or ¼ cup sifted cocoa into the sugar.

2. Mocha Icing – Stir 2 tablespoons sifted cocoa and 1½ teaspoons instant coffee powder into the icing sugar.

Notes:

DIRECTIONS:

In a mixing bowl, beat the cream cheese, butter and vanilla with a large spoon or an electric mixer at medium speed until smooth.

Gradually beat in the sugar until well blended.

Us a knife or a spatula to spread the icing.

Damper

Makes two 15cm (6in) dampers
Preheat the oven to 200°C (400°F)

INGREDIENTS:

2 cups self-raising flour
2 tablespoons butter
1 cup milk
Extra plain flour

Notes:

DIRECTIONS:

Put flour into bowl.

Cut butter into small pieces and using the back of a spoon, rub into flour until it resembles bread crumbs.

Pour in almost all of the milk and mix quickly.

Turn onto a floured surface and knead.

Cut the dough in half. Knead lightly again.

Press each piece of dough to 2cm (¾in) thickness.

Use a sharp knife and indent the top with a cross.

Place on a baking tray (cookie sheet) lined with baking paper, leaving enough space between them to allow for expansion.

Brush top with remainder of the milk and dust with plain flour.

Bake for about 20 minutes or until golden brown.

Earl Grey Tea Cakes

Makes 12
Preheat the oven to 180°C (355°F)

INGREDIENTS:

Melted butter for greasing
2 Earl Grey tea bags
¼ cup boiling water
⅓ cup milk
100g (3½oz) butter (at room temperature)
2 eggs
⅔ cup caster sugar
1¼ cup self-raising flour

Notes:

DIRECTIONS:

Brush 12 medium muffin pans with melted butter to lightly grease.

Empty the tea leaves from the tea bags into a cup and add boiling water.

Set aside for 3 minutes.

Stir in the milk and transfer to a large bowl.

Add the butter, eggs, sugar and flour to tea mixture. Beat until mixture is pale and creamy (the mixture may look slightly curdled).

Spoon the mixture evenly into the greased pans.

Bake for 20-22 minutes or until golden.

Note: This recipe can be used as a whole cake instead by using a 20cm (8in) cake pan and baking at 180°C (355°F) for 40-45 minutes.

Easy Orange Poppy Seed Cake

Makes one 20cm (8in) cake
Preheat the oven to 180ºC (355ºF)

INGREDIENTS:

1½ cups sifted plain flour
1 cup sugar
2 teaspoons baking powder
40g (1½oz) poppy seeds
¾ cup milk
85g (3oz) butter or margarine, cut into small pieces
1 egg
1 teaspoon orange essence or zest of one large orange

Notes:

DIRECTIONS:

Grease and flour a 20cm (8in) square cake tin.

Put the flour, sugar, baking powder, poppy seeds, milk, butter, egg and orange into a mixing bowl. Beat the ingredients together for 3 minutes, or until well blended.

Pour the mixture into the tin and bake, uncovered, for 35 minutes.

Cool in the tin on a wire rack for 10 minutes, then transfer the cake from the tin to the rack and let cool completely.

If you wish, frost the cake with Cream Cheese Icing or Butter Cream Icing.

Easy Shortbread

Makes 20 to 24 biscuits
Preheat the oven to 180ºC (355ºF)

INGREDIENTS:

300g (10½oz) plain flour
100g (3½oz) caster sugar
200g (7oz) unsalted butter, softened to room temperature
Caster sugar for dusting

Notes:

DIRECTIONS:

Place the flour, sugar and butter in the bowl and mix on low speed, increasing to medium speed as the fat breaks up, and until a soft dough is formed.

Be patient – this takes a few minutes and the butter must be at room temperature before you start.

On a lightly floured surface, roll into a long sausage approximately 40cm (16in) long.

Then cut off 1cm (⅜in) thick pieces to form biscuits.

Place on a baking tray (cookie sheet) lined with baking paper.

Bake for 15-20 minutes or until light golden brown.

Dust with additional caster sugar and cool thoroughly before serving.

EJ's Cheesy Hot Cakes

Serves 4 to 6

INGREDIENTS:

1 egg
1 cup self-raising flour (or 1 cup plain flour and 2 teaspoons baking powder)
1 cup cold water (or milk)
2 tablespoons olive oil
½ cup grated tasty cheese

Variations:

1. If you like thicker hot cakes use ¾ cup cold water or milk.
2. Use ¾ cup buttermilk instead of water or milk.

Notes:

DIRECTIONS:

Beat the egg lightly and add all ingredients into a medium-sized mixing bowl. Stir just enough to moisten the mixture – it is OK if it is lumpy. The lumps will cook out.

Set aside to rest for 10 to 15 minutes.

Heat nonstick pan to the point where water just boils (test by dropping a few drops of water on the pan).

Use a jug or ladle to pour about 2 to 3 tablespoons worth for each pancake.

Allow plenty of room because they will spread.

When bubbles show through, they are ready to be turned.

Cook the other side until golden brown.

Serve with butter. (EJ's Cheesy Hot Cakes go well with sausages and scrambled eggs.)

EJ's Magic Hot Cakes

Serves 4 to 6

INGREDIENTS:

1 egg
1 cup self-raising flour (or 1 cup plain flour and 2 teaspoons baking powder)
1 cup cold water (or milk)
2 tablespoons olive oil
¼ cup sugar

Variations:

1. If you like thicker hot cakes use ¾ cup cold water or milk.

2. Use ¾ cup buttermilk instead of water or milk.

Notes:

DIRECTIONS:

Beat the egg lightly and put all the ingredients into a medium-sized mixing bowl. Stir them just enough to moisten the mixture – it is OK if it is lumpy. The lumps will cook out.

Set the mixture aside for 10 to 15 minutes.

Heat a nonstick pan to the point where water just boils (test by dropping a few drops of water on the pan).

Use a jug or ladle to pour about 2 to 3 tablespoons worth for each pancake.

Allow plenty of room because they will spread.

When bubbles show through, they are ready to be turned.

Cook the other side until golden brown.

Serve with butter. (EJ's Magic Hot Cakes go well with sausages or crispy bacon and scrambled eggs.)

Family-Style Gingerbread Person

Makes 16
Preheat the oven to 180ºC (355ºF)

INGREDIENTS - Biscuits:

125g (4½oz) unsalted butter
⅓ cup soft dark brown or soft brown sugar
¼ cup golden syrup
1 egg, lightly beaten
2 cups plain flour
¼ cup self-raising flour
1 tablespoon ground ginger
1 teaspoon bicarbonate of soda
1 tablespoon currants

INGREDIENTS - Icing:

1 egg white
½ teaspoon lemon juice
1¼ cups icing sugar, sifted
Assorted food colourings

Notes:

DIRECTIONS - Biscuits:

Line two or three baking trays (cookie sheets) with baking paper.

Using electric beaters, beat the butter, sugar and syrup in small mixing bowl until light and creamy. Add the egg gradually, beating thoroughly after each addition. Transfer the mixture to a large bowl.

With the exception of currants, sift the dry ingredients onto butter mixture. Mix with a knife until it is just combined. Combine the dough with well-floured hands. (See Hygiene) Turn the dough onto a well-floured surface and knead it for 1-2 minutes or until smooth.

Line a large chopping board with baking paper. Roll out the dough onto the board to 5mm thickness. (Flour your rolling pin if necessary to prevent sticking.)

Refrigerate the dough on the board for 15 minutes so it is firm to cut.

Cut the dough into shapes with a 13cm (5in) gingerbread person cutter. Press the remaining dough together and re-roll. Cut out additional shapes.

Place the biscuits on the prepared trays. Use the currants for eyes and noses on the gingerbread persons.

Bake for 10 minutes or until lightly browned. Cool the biscuits on the trays.

Decorate your gingerbread persons with icing when they are cool to cold.

DIRECTIONS - Icing:

Place the egg white in a small dry mixing bowl. Beat the egg white until they are foamy. Add the lemon juice and icing sugar gradually. Beat the mixture until it is thick and creamy.

Divide the mixture into several bowls. Tint them each with different food colourings. (Caution: use only a drop of colour at a time because a little colour goes a long way.)

Spoon the mixture into small paper icing bags, sealing the open ends. Snip the tips off the piping bags. Pipe faces and clothing onto your gingerbread persons.

Gingerbread Cake

Makes 1 23cm (9in) cake
Preheat the oven to 180ºC (355ºF)

INGREDIENTS:

125g (4½oz) butter or margarine
¾ cup dark treacle
½ cup firmly packed brown sugar
½ cup milk
2 cups self-raising flour
1 teaspoon ground ginger
1 teaspoon ground mixed spices
½ teaspoon bicarbonate of soda
2 eggs, well beaten

Notes:

DIRECTIONS:

Line the bottom and sides of a 23cm (9in), square or round, cake pan with baking paper.

Put the butter, treacle and sugar into a small saucepan over low heat, melt the butter, then add the milk and stir.

Put the saucepan on one side to cool.

Meanwhile, sift the flour, ginger, mixed spices, and bicarbonate of soda into a mixing bowl.

Add the eggs and mix well, then add the cool butter mixture and stir it all together until well combined.

Pour the batter into the cake pan and bake until it is firm to the touch — about 30 to 35 minutes.

Allow the gingerbread cake to cool in the pan before turning out onto a wire cooling rack.

Serve plain or buttered.

Karen's Chocolate Simplicity Cake

Makes one 20cm (8in) two-layer cake
Preheat the oven to 180ºC (355ºF)

INGREDIENTS:

3 tablespoons butter
2 tablespoons cocoa
1 cup self-raising flour
1 cup sugar
½ cup milk
2 eggs
½ teaspoon vanilla

Serving suggestion:

When the cakes are completely cool, place one layer on a cake stand or suitable flat plate or board. Spread a layer of whipped cream on top and then place the other cake on top.

The cake can be iced or left as is. Another variation is to add strawberry jam on the top of the bottom layer with the cream.

If you wish, ice the cake with Cream Cheese Icing or Butter Cream Icing, or there are a number of ready-made icings available at your supermarket.

Notes:

DIRECTIONS:

Line the bottom of 2 x 20cm (8in) pans with baking paper.

Melt the butter.

Put all the other ingredients into a large bowl and pour the melted butter on top.

Using an electric beater, beat on medium for 3 minutes.

Pour mixture into the prepared tins and place in the middle of the oven for 35 minutes or until the top springs back when lightly touched with a finger. Alternately when a skewer inserted in the centre comes out clean.

When baked, allow cakes to cool in the baking tins for 10 minutes.

After ten minutes, carefully run a knife around the sides of the tin and then, placing your hand over the cake (See Hygiene), turn it upside down. The cake should slide out.

Place right side up on a wire rack to cool.

Killer Chocolate Cookies

Makes 24
Preheat the oven to 170°C (340°F)

INGREDIENTS:

220g (8oz) plain flour
60g (2oz) cocoa powder
1 teaspoon bicarbonate of soda
340g (12oz) plain dark chocolate broken into pieces
340g (12oz) dark brown sugar
170g (6oz) unsalted butter
2 eggs
1 teaspoon vanilla essence

Notes:

DIRECTIONS:

Line two baking trays (cookie sheets) with baking paper.

Sift together the flour, cocoa powder, and bicarbonate of soda into a dry bowl. Set the bowl aside.

Heat 3cm (1in) of water in the bottom half of a double boiler over medium heat. Place the chocolate in the top half of the double boiler. Cover and allow the chocolate to heat for 10 minutes. Remove the pan from the heat and stir until smooth. Keep the chocolate at room temperature until it is needed.

Beat the dark brown sugar and butter with an electric mixer on medium until creamy.

Scrape down the bowl half way through.

Add the eggs, one at a time, while beating on medium, and stopping to scrape down the bowl after incorporating each addition.

Add the vanilla essence and the melted chocolate and beat on low until combined.

Add the sifted flour, cocoa powder, and bicarbonate of soda and beat on low until thoroughly combined.

Remove the bowl from the mixer and mix thoroughly with a spoon.

Drop 1 heaped teaspoon of mixture per biscuit onto each of the 2 baking trays.

Allow plenty of space between biscuits to allow for spreading.

Put the biscuits on the top and middle shelves of the preheated oven and bake for 18 minutes, rotating the sheets from top to bottom about halfway through the baking time.

Allow the biscuits to cool for 5 to 6 minutes on the baking sheets.

Transfer the biscuits to a cooling rack to cool thoroughly before serving or storing in a sealed plastic container.

Lazy Day Golden Cake

Makes 1 two-layer 20cm (8in) cake
Preheat the oven to 180°C (355°F)

INGREDIENTS:

1½ cups sifted plain flour
1 cup sugar
2 teaspoons baking powder
¾ cup milk
85g (3oz) butter or margarine, cut into small pieces
1 egg
1 teaspoon vanilla essence

Notes:

DIRECTIONS:

Line the bottoms of 2 x 20cm (8in) round cake tins with baking paper.

Put the flour, sugar, baking powder, milk, butter, egg and vanilla into a mixing bowl.

Beat the ingredients together for 3 minutes, or until they are well blended. (Do not over mix.)

Pour the mixture into the cake tins and bake them for 35 minutes.

Cool in the tins on a wire rack for 10 minutes.

After 10 minutes carefully run a knife around the sides of each tin and then, placing your hand over the cake, turn it upside down. The cake should slide out.

Place the cakes right side up on a wire rack to cool.

Serving suggestion: When the cakes are completely cool, place one on a cake stand or suitable flat plate or board. Spread a layer of whipped cream on top and then place the other cake on top of that.

The cake can be iced or left as is. Another variation is to add strawberry jam on the top of the bottom layer with the cream.

If you wish, frost the cake with Cream Cheese Icing or Butter Cream Icing, or there are a number of ready-made frostings available at your supermarket.

Lemon Self-Saucing Pudding

Serves 4
Preheat the oven to 180°C (355°F)

INGREDIENTS:

3 eggs, separated
60g (2oz) butter or margarine
¾ cup sugar
Grated zest of 1 lemon
½ cup lemon juice
1 cup milk
¼ cup unsifted plain flour

While baking, the pudding sinks to the bottom and the cake rises to the top. The result resembles a lemon pie but is far easier to make.

Notes:

DIRECTIONS:

In a mixing bowl, beat the whites of the eggs until they form stiff peaks, and then put them aside.

In a separate bowl, cream the butter and sugar until it is light and fluffy. Beat in the lemon zest, lemon juice and the egg yolks, one at a time, until it is all well mixed.

Beat in the milk, then the flour, until blended.

Fold the beaten egg whites into the lemon mixture, then pour the mixture into a greased 20cm (8in) shallow casserole dish.

Set the dish into a larger pan; pour hot water into the outer pan to a level of about 2cm (¾in).

Bake, uncovered, for 35 minutes. Serve warm or cold.

Luscious Cheesy Things

Makes 10
Preheat the oven to 200ºC (400ºF)

INGREDIENTS:

2¼ cups self-raising flour
200g (7oz) tasty cheese (finely grated)
¼ cup olive oil
1 egg, lightly beaten
½ cup soy milk

Notes:

DIRECTIONS:

With the back of a spoon, rub grated cheese through the flour.

Combine the lightly beaten egg with the olive oil and the soy milk.

Make a well in the centre of the dry mixture and pour in the liquid.

Stir with the flat side of a knife until well combined, then knead briefly until the pastry is smooth.

Roll the dough out to 2cm (¾in) thick on a floured surface.

Cut out the cheesy things using a 5cm (2in) scone cutter (cookie or biscuit cutter).

Place them on a baking tray (cookie sheet) covered with baking paper. Make sure they are touching so they will rise rather than spread.

Place the tray in the middle of the oven and bake for 20 minutes or until cheesy things are golden brown.

When they are baked, take them out of the oven and allow them to cool on the baking tray.

They can be served hot or cold with lashings (lots and lots) of butter.

Parmesan Biscuits

Makes 30
Preheat the oven to moderate 180ºC (355ºF)

INGREDIENTS:

150g (5oz) unsalted butter
¾ cup grated Parmesan cheese
⅓ cup grated cheddar cheese
1¼ cups plain flour, sifted
2 teaspoons lemon pepper seasoning
¼ cup sunflower seeds
¼ cup grated Parmesan cheese

Notes:

DIRECTIONS:

Line two baking trays (cookie sheets) with baking paper.

Beat the butter until it is light and creamy.

Add ¾ cup of Parmesan and ⅓ cup of cheddar cheese and beat until they are combined.

Sift the flour and seasoning.

Fold in, using a metal spoon.

Now add the sunflower seeds.

Combine mixture with well-floured hands.

Turn onto a lightly floured surface and knead for 2-3 minutes or until smooth.

Roll out the dough between two sheets of baking paper to 5mm (¼ in) thickness.

Cut it into squares, using a floured 4cm square (1½in) biscuit cutter (cookie cutter).

Place the squares on the prepared trays, allowing room for spreading.

Sprinkle the top of each biscuit with a little extra Parmesan cheese.

Bake for 10-15 minutes or until golden. Allow the biscuits to cool on trays.

Pavlova

Serves 6 to 8
Preheat the oven to 120°C (250°F)

INGREDIENTS:

4 egg whites
1 cup caster sugar
1 tablespoon cornflour
1 teaspoon white vinegar
300ml (10½oz) carton thickened cream
2 teaspoons vanilla essence
1 tablespoon icing sugar
Fruit of your choice, to serve

Notes:

DIRECTIONS:

Cover a baking tray (cookie sheet) with baking paper, and with a pencil, mark an 18cm (7in) circle on the paper.

Beat the egg whites in a small bowl with an electric mixer until soft peaks form.

Gradually add the caster sugar, beating it until dissolved after each addition.

Fold in the cornflour and vinegar. Spread meringue inside the circle on the prepared tray. For best results, do not squash or flatten the mixture but shape the sides up and in towards the centre, like a mound. Make furrows up the sides using a small spatula, then level the top.

Bake the meringue in a very slow oven for about 1¼ hours or until dry to the touch. Turn the oven off and leave meringue to cool in the oven with the door ajar.

An hour before serving, beat the cream with the vanilla essence and icing sugar until soft peaks form. Fill the meringue with the cream mixture and decorate with fruit.

Quick Rice Pudding

Serves 6

INGREDIENTS:

½ teaspoon salt
2 cups water
1 cup uncooked rice
1 cup raisins (optional)
¼ cup firmly packed brown sugar
1 cup chopped walnuts (optional)
1 cup thickened cream
¼ teaspoon ground cinnamon
2 teaspoons lemon juice

You can do most of the preparation while the rice cooks. Or use about 3 cups leftover cooked rice and assemble the pudding in 5 minutes.

Notes:

DIRECTIONS:

Bring the salt and water to a boil in a 2 litre (2 quart) saucepan. Add the rice, stir once, reduce the heat, cover, and simmer for 15 minutes.

Remove the pan from heat and let it stand covered for 10 minutes.

Meanwhile, in a mixing bowl, combine the raisins, sugar, walnuts, cream, cinnamon and lemon juice.

Add the warm rice to the ingredients in the bowl and stir to mix.

Serve warm or cold.

Singe's Infamous and Special Peanut Butter Cookies

Makes 24
Preheat the oven to 180°C (355°F)

INGREDIENTS:

½ cup butter
½ cup caster sugar
½ cup soft brown sugar
½ cup peanut butter (smooth or crunchy)
1 egg
1¼ cups plain flour
½ teaspoon baking powder
¾ teaspoon bicarbonate of soda
Pinch of salt

Notes:

DIRECTIONS:

Line a baking tray (cookie sheet) with baking paper.

Thoroughly mix together the butter, caster sugar, brown sugar, egg and peanut butter in a bowl.

When it is all mixed, add the flour, baking powder, salt and bicarb and mix it all thoroughly together.

Place heaped teaspoons of the mixture on the baking sheet making sure to leave enough space for spreading.

Put indents in the top surface with a fork.

Place the baking tray in the oven and bake until the cookies are golden brown.

Allow them to cool on the tray for five minutes and then transfer them to a wire rack to cool completely.

Store in an airtight cookie jar or storage container.

Traditional Aussie Scones

Makes 12
Preheat the oven to 220°C (425°F)

INGREDIENTS:

3 cups self-raising flour
1 tablespoon caster sugar
80g (2½oz) butter, chopped
1 cup milk (for buttermilk scones use 1 cup buttermilk instead)

<u>*Notes:*</u>

DIRECTIONS:

Line a baking tray (cookie sheet) with baking paper.

Sift the flour into a medium bowl, then add the sugar.

Using your fingertips, rub the butter into flour mixture until it resembles fine bread crumbs. (See Hygiene)

Add the milk, then use a flat-bladed knife or spatula to mix it in until the dough begins to come together.

Turn the dough onto a lightly floured surface and knead gently until it comes together.

Flatten the dough with the palm of your hand until it is 2cm (¾in) thick. Use a 5cm (2in) scone cutter (cookie or biscuit cutter) or a glass of a similar size to cut out scones.

Place them onto a baking tray 1cm apart.

Bake for 14-16 minutes until golden and cooked through.

Serve warm with jam and thick cream.

Traditional Scottish Shortbread

Makes 12 biscuits
Preheat the oven to 180°C (355°F)

INGREDIENTS:

1⅛ cups plain flour
125g (4½oz) soft unsalted butter
¾ cup cornflour
¼ cup caster sugar
1 egg, beaten
1 tablespoon cream
Caster sugar for dusting

Notes:

DIRECTIONS:

Place the plain flour and butter in a warmed bowl and, using your hands, rub butter into flour until mixture resembles bread crumbs. (See Hygiene)

Add the cornflour, sugar, egg and cream and mix until a stiff dough is formed.

On a lightly floured surface roll out the dough to 1½cm (1in) thick and cut it into 6cm rounds using a pastry cutter.

Arrange the rounds on a baking tray (cookie sheet) covered with baking paper and lightly prick the surface of each round three or four times with a dinner fork.

Bake for 30 minutes or until light golden brown.

Dust with additional caster sugar and cool thoroughly before serving.

13248281R00106

Printed in Great Britain
by Amazon